Bitcoin Trading 2021 – 2 Books in 1

Discover the Best Trading Strategies to to Build Wealth During the 2021 Bull Run (Futures, Options, DCA, Swing Trading and Day Trading Strategies Included!)

Cryptocurrency Trading for Beginners

Learn the Basics of Fundamental Analysis and the 13 Candlestick Patterns to Make Money Trading Bitcoin and other Crypto in the 2021 Bull Run

By

Charles Swing

&

Masaru Nakamoto

damages that may befall them after undertaking information described herein.

Additionally, the information in the following pages is intended only for informational purposes and should thus be thought of as universal. As befitting its nature, it is presented without assurance regarding its prolonged validity or interim quality. Trademarks that are mentioned are done without written consent and can in no way be considered an endorsement from the trademark holder.

Table of Contents

5

Introduction

Bitcoin has taken the world by storm once again when it crossed $20,000 per BTC in December of last year.

A lot of people are trying to improvise themselves as professional traders and are losing a lot of money, only helping those who actually know what they are doing accumulate an incredible amount of wealth.

To join the club of the few traders that actually make it, you need the right strategies and the right mindset. Notice how we did not include a large initial capital. In fact, while having more money to trade with means having more fire power, it is not necessary to have thousands of dollars to be profitable and build wealth.

In fact, when we started trading cryptocurrencies we only had a few hundreds to put into the market, but that sum yielded us thousands and thousands of dollars.

In this book you are going to discover all the strategies that have allowed us to take our trading skills to the next level. If you apply them diligently we are sure you are going to see amazing results in a relative short period of time.

Please, stay away from all the shiny objects of the cryptocurrency world. Just choose one cryptocurrency pair, study it deeply and then milk it like a cash cow!

To your success!

Chapter 1 - Fundamental Analysis and Cryptocurrencies

The time has come to look at real trading strategies that you can apply to make money trading cryptocurrencies. Basically, there are two types of analysis when it comes to trading: fundamental and technical analysis. We are going to cover both these methodologies in this book, but please make sure to understand one simple concept. When you are trading cryptocurrencies (trading, not investing), we highly recommend that you take into consideration technical patterns much more than fundamental news. In fact, after studying and operating in this market for over 5 years, we have come to the conclusion that technical indicators play a much bigger role than news.

Therefore, we have decided to dedicate a brief chapter on fundamental analysis, before moving on to the different patterns that can give you a sense of where the market is going.

Bitcoin and cryptocurrency trading has spread like wildfires in recent years. This is thanks to the charm that virtual currency generates (either because it is a novelty in the currency landscape or for the sense of independence that characterizes it) but also of the extraordinary market performance. The Bitcoin market, despite a certain underlying volatility, is booming but this does not mean that trading it is easy. Indeed, some specific elements of this cryptocurrency intervene to complicate the trading activity. In fact, there are some characteristics that are not found in traditional currencies and that make traders face greater difficulties. All this generates some difficulties in the practice of disciplines that have always given substance to the speculative investment experience. The reference is, in particular, to fundamental analysis. Doing the fundamental analysis for Bitcon is different from doing it for any other traditional currency, be it the dollar, the euro, the pound or the yen.

Yet fundamental analysis cannot be given up completely, even if trading cryptocurrencies. Therefore, it is necessary to understand how this irreplaceable discipline is expressed in the context of cryptocurrencies. In this chapter we will talk about the relationship between fundamental analysis and Bitcoin, starting from an overview of the fundamental analysis itself up to providing some useful and practical advice.

Why fundamental analysis?

For some, the more experienced or for those who have long passed the beginner stage, it is a rhetorical question. In fact, fundamental analysis is an integrated part of the trading experience, an invaluable tool, a resource whose use really represents a fundamental tool to trade better.

Fundamental analysis is the study of what is happening in the market with the goal of forecasting the trend or the prices using news. Those who practice fundamental analysis follow the events that can affect the price of an asset, in this case the value of a cryptocurrency, and try to react accordingly. These events, which are mostly cyclical, are called market movers. For example, the FED's interest rate announcement is a crucial market mover for the dollar, as the manipulation of rates directly affects the money supply and therefore its value relative to other currencies. Predicting the content of the announcement - or guessing it from the economic conditions, the historian and the approaches of the board - means knowing with a good degree of approximation the near future of the dollar.

All currencies have their own market movers. Some are outspoken, well researched in the literature and in the spotlight, such as those related to central banks. The presence of a strong institution capable of influencing the market, however counterintuitive the concept may be, is a positive fact as it makes the currencies themselves very readable.

There are market movers of different nature. Among the most important, for currencies, are those related to the real economy.

It is obvious that the dollar is linked to the economy of the US, so if the latter is growing, this will also affect the currency.

Does fundamental analysis work with Bitcon?

The question is more a provocation than anything else, also because at a superficial glance it would seem easy to think that it is impossible to do fundamental analysis with Bitcoinn.

The reasons are easy to understand. We have said that much of the fundamental analysis in the currency field is based on the study of market movers concerning the activity of central banks and the underlying real economy. But, in hindsight, Bitcoin has no such entities.

Bitcoin, like all cryptocurrencies, is headless. It does not enjoy the support of an institution that, in some way, can regulate its offer, manage critical issues and resolve emergencies.

The dollar, when it appreciated in a way that was harmful to the US, was the subject of an ultra-expansive monetary policy which decreased its value. The currencies of developing countries, which are at risk of devaluation due to heavy domestic inflation, regularly experience ultra-tight monetary policy.

This is true for all traditional currencies, but not for Bitcoin. There is no central bank. Therefore, the fundamental market mover is missing. To tell the truth, as we have seen in the first chapters, there is a supply regulation mechanism, but it is practically automatic and cannot make decisions on its own. Consequently, Bitcoin is not tied to any national economy. It is a global currency, with an internationalist vocation, a feature that made it interesting right from the start. However, the biggest negative consequence remains that there are zero market movers linked to the real economy.

If we take into consideration these elements and the absence of a link with a real economy, it makes us want to throw in the towel, and admit that no fundamental analysis can be done on Bitcoin.

However, what emerges from a more in-depth analysis is very different.

Bitcoin market movers

Bitcoin enjoys some market movers, which are not tied to a central bank or a real economy. They are not direct market movers, but indirect market movers. To find them, it is necessary to understand which event is able to affect the price of Bitcoin. This event is the association of Bitcoin with the concept of "safe haven". Let us be clear, this only applies to the current historical period, the association may change in the future.

Now, it remains to ask which events, therefore which market movers, can mark Bitcoin's approach to this status. The answer is all in all simple: those market movers that suggest a loss of prestige on the part of assets traditionally considered "safe-haven assets". Specifically, gold (or precious metals), the dollar and other fiat currencies.

Here is revealed the secret of Bitcoin on a fundamental level. Everything that establishes a difficulty for gold, the dollar and other major currencies is a market mover for Bitcoin, specifically in a bullish sense. For instance, sudden cut in central bank rates, banking crisis, mining crisis of the precious metal are events that can trigger a bullish run in Bitcoin's price.

But there is more. So far we have talked about market movers linked to the real economy and monetary policy. Yet, among the most powerful market movers, important policy makers stand out. They impose a perspective to the entire market, anticipate future evolutions and, in fact, push traders to action. In this case, we are referring to governments and regulators. If they announce that they are going to strict the rules regarding cryptocurrencies, you can expect the price to fall.

Actually, these entities have never succeeded in suppressing the price for a long period of time, since the price has always gone back up. Funny enough, there is a site, called 99Bitcoins where you can see how many times the cryptocurrency has been declared dead (https://99bitcoins.com/bitcoin-obituaries/).

Now that we have discussed the role of fundamental analysis in predicting the cryptocurrency market, we can dive deeper into technical analysis and see which trading strategies you can implement to assure your success in this market.

Chapter 2 - Cryptocurrencies and Technical Analysis

In this chapter we are going to discuss the basic concepts of technical analysis and it will serve as a starting point for the strategies presented in the rest of the book.

Let's start by discussing what technical analysis is, as it is important to understand its basics before diving deeper into the different indicators and strategies.

When you read the following pages, please take into consideration the fact that technical analysis can be applied to almost every market out there, not only crypto. This means that if you study this content very well, you will have the chance to become a good trader not only in the cryptocurrency market. In fact, we are sure you are going to get good results when trading almost every asset class.

In economics, technical analysis is the study of the price trend of financial markets over time, with the aim of predicting future trends, mainly using graphical and statistical methods. In a broad sense, it is that theory of analysis (or set of principles and tools) according to which it is possible to predict the future trend of the price of a listed asset, by studying its past history. It is used, together with fundamental analysis, for the definition of financial operational decisions.

The technical analysis aims to analyze and understand, through the analysis of the graph, the trend of prices, which in turn reflects the decisions of investors and traders. Moreover, it is based on the fundamental assumption that, since investor behavior is repeated over time, upon the occurrence of certain graphic conditions, prices will also move accordingly.

Originally, technical analysis was only applied to the stock market, but its spread has gradually involved the commodity, bond, cryptocurrency and other international markets.

The study of the movement of financial markets includes the three main sources of information available to the analyst: price, volume and open interest. The term "price movement" is therefore limited for a technical analyst who also considers volumes and open interest as integral parts of the market analysis. However, it is a study at the basis of speculative movements which has always been considered in contrast with the study of structural aspects of the real economy (fundamental analysis, as we have seen in the previous chapter).

Therefore, the main task of technical analysis is to identify a trend change from an early stage, holding an investment position until there is evidence that the trend itself has reversed again. The traders who will apply it will have a clearly different view from those who will instead apply a simpler and more common technique called buy and hold. This approach, which is very popular in the crypto world, consists in buying and holding the position for a long time. There is a lively debate regarding the best trading strategy, which must always be carefully implemented based on the investor's goals, availability and risk appetite compared to the expected return.

A dynamic and short-term investment strategy based on frequent trading to exploit the volatility of the markets based only on technical analysis presents on average a greater risk in the search for possible higher returns. On the contrary, a more conservative investment strategy (buy and hold based on fundamental analysis, with a medium-long term vision) usually presents lower risks and lower returns.

The possible advantages of technical analysis compared to the buy and hold strategy are particularly evident in periods in which the markets do not register any progress or net trend. The most striking cases that can be remembered are those of the Dow Jones Industrial Average index during the period 1966-1982. At the end of 1982, the value of the index differed slightly from that reached in 1966. However, during this time the DJIA registered 5 bullish cycles. A hypothetical trader who (rather unlikely anyway) was brave enough to sell at the five highs and buy at the lows, would have seen his capital grow from $1,000 in 1966 to $10,000 by October 1983. In the same period, an investor that applied the buy-and-hold strategy would only have earned $250.

Another example is the trend of the Comit index from 1973 to 1996. The decade 1986-1996 appears particularly significant, during which the index did not register any progress. In this period a buy and hold strategy would have recorded an even negative performance, while a strategy that had dynamically and always correctly identified the main turning points would have made gains more likely.

One last example can be taken from the world of crypto. From January 2018 to December 2020, Bitcoin moved in a range between $20,000 and $3000. If you had actively traded the market using the strategies presented in this book, you would have made much more money than just buying the asset and storing it in your wallet.

However, it is necessary to avoid the illusion of easy gains resulting automatically from the use of technical analysis, because in the reality of trading it is obviously unthinkable to be able to buy exactly at the lower points and sell at the higher points without making mistakes. These values can obviously only be known ex post in historical studies. Therefore, the purpose of technical analysis is to help improve the identification of the direction of a trend, and to signal when its reversal is close. Since it is impossible to conceive a single instrument capable of signaling all the turning points, many have been built, which are not limited only to graphical indicators, but also to quantitative and statistical ones.

In general terms, these instruments are a set of indicators, defined as functions of previous prices and volumes; the achievement of a certain predetermined value as a threshold signals the opportunity of a purchase or a sale. In the overwhelming majority of cases these are procedures developed and refined in the United States since the 1930s, and which over the course of over seventy years have determined sets of rules that constitute a concentration of operational experiences of thousands of operators; such rules are often implemented in so-called automated "trading systems".

Basic assumptions of technical analysis

The assumptions on which technical analysis bases its forecasts are essentially the following three.

- **The price discounts everything**

21

This statement is a basic premise for the correct understanding of technical analysis. In fact, the analyst moves from the belief that all the fundamental factors (political, psychological, monetary and economic), are already incorporated in the prices of the cryptocurrency market.

The charts, in fact, by themselves do not make the market go up or down, but simply reflect its bullish or bearish psychology.

Since the technical approach may seem somewhat simplistic, the premise "the market discounts everything" gains strength with individual experience and demonstrates that the study of market prices is a fundamental element of technical analysis. By studying the graphs, supported by technical indicators, analysts are able to understand which direction the market intends to take, without having to resort to the analysis of the reasons external to the price itself.

- **History repeats itself**

This is very evident in situations such as double highs or lows, or situations in which prices stop their bullish or bearish run in the proximity of price ranges that had previously reversed current trends, demonstrating how some critical price points can be remembered by traders even after years.

- **Validity of trends**

Given the previous point, it is easier for a trend to have a standard direction than an abrupt reversal, and it can therefore be said that the trend is destined to continue until it shows clear signs of reversal.

In addition to the three factors indicated above, it is good to clarify and evaluate the hypothesis of market inefficiency and the hypothesis of irrational behavior on the part of the various operators.

Some criticisms of the technical approach

Over time, with the widespread popularization of technical analysis around the world, a number of objections have emerged regarding the technical approach to cryptocurrency markets. The main points are those of self-limitation, due to the similar behavior of numerous operators, and that of predicting the direction of future prices by using only past data. In fact, critics usually argue that graphs say where the market is, but they can't say where it will go.

First of all, it should be emphasized that, if one is not able to interpret it adequately, a graph will never be able to give useful information.

It should also be remembered the random walk theory, which argues that prices move in a random direction, and therefore a forecasting technique can only be reduced to a bet. Obviously this is not a criticism only of technical analysis, but of any study aimed at identifying the future direction of the markets.

Self-feeding theory

The spread of technical analysis to an increasing number of people has meant that many operators have excellent preparation and a good familiarity with the use of indicators. This means, according to this theory, that there are masses of capital moved accordingly, creating waves of purchases and sales in response to bullish or bearish indicators.

However, it should be remembered that the identification of the patterns is absolutely a subjective factor, and no study has so far been able to quantify them mathematically. In fact, in front of the same graph many traders can give multiple analyzes and identify different patterns. Interpretation is therefore partly subjective, and reading a graph is considered an art, even if it would be more correct to speak of a skill. The technical patternsare rarely obvious, so that even experienced analysts are often not in agreement in their interpretations. On the other hand, if this removes the idea that the same pattern identified by several operators can lead to mass movements, it certainly casts a shadow on the predictivity of the method, given that the same trend can produce, depending on the analyst, completely different outcomes.

In addition to all these considerations, it is necessary to take into account the different approach to the market that all operators have. In fact, some would certainly try to anticipate the technical pattern, others would buy or sell on the "breaking" of a given figure, others would still wait for confirmation of the signal before taking a stand. Therefore the possibility of all analysts acting at the same time and in the same way is very remote.

Much more worrying is the strong growth in the use of computerized technical systems (trading systems) in the futures market. Therefore, it often happens with these wealth management systems that a huge mass of money is concentrated on a small number of trends. This actually leads to slight distortions of price movements in the short term, even if they fail to change a primary market trend.

Efficient market hypothesis
Another question that often arises concerns the validity of using past prices to predict future prices. The efficient market hypothesis, one of the most solidly verified assumptions of scientific economics over the years, implies that it is not possible to use historical price series to predict prices in an advantageous way. The basic assumption of this hypothesis is that the market is much quicker to respond to changes in the conditions in

which prices are determined than the single trader in possession of incomplete information. Note that this hypothesis does not exclude the possibility of predicting prices, but implies that the advance of the forecast with respect to the variation is statistically irrelevant for the purposes of financial revenue.

To the objection often raised by technical analysts, according to which real traders are not as rational as the efficient market hypothesis assumes, the statistical argument is contrasted. In fact, if it is true that the single trader can act irrationally, globally the deviations from rational behavior will be distributed symmetrically, so as to balance itself. Therefore, the result is a global effect not unlike that which would occur in the presence of only rational traders, albeit with greater statistical dispersion.

One consequence of the efficient market hypothesis (in a weaker form) is that the recognition of patterns by technical analysts can lead to the invalidation of the patterns themselves. In fact, once participants are aware of the presence of patterns connected to certain trends, their collective action will prevent them from occurring in the future. This interpretation was proposed by the Princeton economist, Burton Malkiel.

The response of technical analysts is typically linked to the notion that price trends represent a kind of collective psychological effect of non-rational traders. While on the one hand this exposes the risk of identifying missing correlations of a fundamental scientific explanation, on the other it could account for the fact that, although technical analysis is often based on idiosyncrasies of dubious analysts, there is still growing evidence of informational advantage for its users.

Indicators and oscillators

Numerous tools (indicators and oscillators) have been studied and created to help the analyst in the timely identification of trends and the first signs of weakening. To try to give a better idea of how many tools are available, it is worth mentioning that there are over 100 indicators present in some technical analysis software. Do not worry, you do not need to study them all to have good results in the cryptocurrency market.

As you can see, there are different opinions on the usefulness of technical analysis. Our experience tells us that it works particularly well in the cryptocurrency market, especially when trading Bitcoin and major altcoins. Of course, as we have mentioned at the beginning of this chapter, it is unlikely to be able to correctly predict market movements every single time. However, by studying and applying the strategies presented in this book, along with a good money management system, you will be on your way to riches even if a good amount of your operations turns red.

Chapter 3 - Candlesticks

While in the previous chapter we have talked about the basics of technical analysis, now it is time to dive deeper into the topic and start looking at the most important element that constitutes a chart. We are talking about candlesticks and the next pages are going to tell you everything you need to know about them.

Even if you have recently approached cryptocurrency trading, you have already heard of candlesticks. The so-called candlestick trading is a real system of analysis of market charts through a particular representation of prices called, in fact, candles.

We commonly speak of Japanese candles because, as it turns out, the candlestick analysis originated in feudal Japan between the seventeenth and eighteenth centuries. This is, in all likelihood, the oldest method of graphical analysis of the financial markets.

Studying Japanese candlesticks has immediate advantages even for novice traders as this type of graphical representation of prices immediately visually highlights the imbalance of forces between buyers and sellers in every single trading session.

And it is probably for this reason that many cryptocurrency traders use Japanese candlestick trading.

The Japanese candlestick chart is of simple construction and does not require any additional information compared to the classic bar chart.

To construct Japanese candlesticks and identify the main patterns of this methodology, the four summary trading prices (opening, maximum, minimum and closing) are in fact sufficient.

But how do you read Japanese candles?

If you have never learned anything about this topic, take some of your time and read this detailed chapter on Japanese candlesticks.

We will see together how Japanese candlesticks are built and what they mean. We will review what we commonly call 'candlestick patterns' and with candlestick trading we will see how to operate with the main types of Japanese candlesticks.

It will be a very practical path with examples taken from real markets so that the meaning of Japanese candlesticks, their interpretation and understanding of this trading methodology is not confined to the examination of purely theoretical pattenrs.

The construction of the candlestick chart

The construction of the chart using Japanese candlesticks offers, compared to the bar chart, additional information based on the relationship between the first and last traded price, or between the opening and closing data.

Each single candle is in fact made up of the following parts.

- Main or real body ('jittay' in Japanese). This is the body of the candle, which is obtained by combining the opening price with the closing price.

- Shadow ('kage'). These are the thin lines that connect the maximum and minimum (High and Low) of the candle to the body, respectively defined 'upper shadow' ('uwakage') and 'lower shadow' ('shitakage')

Each candle can take on a different color (generally the most used ones are red and green, or black and white) depending on whether the close of the market is higher ('positive session') or lower ('negative session') than the relative opening price.

In the 'default' graphical analysis software, the convention of 'filling' the body of the bearish candle (coloring it black) is often used, leaving, instead, empty (tracing only the outline) the body of the bullish candle, as we can see in the image below.

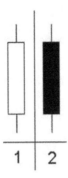

Current software now makes it possible to color the candle bodies in the preferred way to distinguish at a glance the positive ones from the negative ones, i.e. bullish from bearish candles.

As already mentioned in this guide, it is now common practice to use green for candles with a positive trend and red for negative ones.

Thanks to well-defined colors, reading Japanese candles is very simple. When we use a Japanese candlestick chart, in fact, we can clearly see within an uptrend a prevalence of positive green candles while on the contrary in a bearish trend we will notice the predominance of red or negative candles.

How to interpret the Japanese candlestick chart in trading

Candlestick analysis makes it possible to identify nine different types of Japanese candlesticks as a starting point, each of which represents a different movement of the market within the trading session.

Each of them gives rise to a real Japanese candlestick strategy, exploitable from an operational point of view in the way that we will see.

The meaning of Japanese candles and their interpretation primarily concern how they present themselves at the end of the session. That is, what shape the individual candle taken into consideration has taken compared to the previous one.

The shape that the candle takes at the end of the session in fact offers us a lot of information on the progress of the cryptocurrency market session as a whole. This information can be exploited from an operational point of view.

Candlestick trading includes different candlestick patterns based on a single candle or on several candles to be evaluated as a whole.

Before reviewing these patterns, it is necessary to examine these nine types of candles that constitute the basic figures of the analysis with Japanese candlesticks.

1. Long white body

A candle with a very large body has strong bullish implications. The market went in one direction only, that is to the upside.

In fact, after the opening, prices pushed upwards, closing close to the highs recorded in the trading session. In the event that the opening coincides with the minimum of the session and the closing with the maximum, this candle represents the maximum bullish force that a market can express and therefore presents itself without a 'shadow' (or in any case with an almost non-existent 'shadow') . In this case we speak of a 'marubozu' candle.

The presence of this imbalance of forces in favor of the buyers paints a potentially bullish scenario for the immediately following session as well.

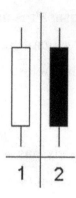

2. Long black body

This is a candlestick with strongly bearish implications. It is a pattern exactly mirroring the previous one and highlights a strong prevalence of sellers over buyers. A high probability of further declines is deduced in the immediately following session.

3. and 4. Small body / spinning top

These candlestick patterns indicate substantial market stability. These candles have a body that is too small to allow for the assessment of the imbalance between buyers and sellers regardless of the color of the individual candle (#3 indicates upside and #4 downside). In forecast terms, these patterns show moderate potential for increases (No. 3) or decreases (No. 4).

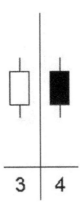

3 | 4

5. and 6. Upper shadow lines

In the Japanese candlestick strategy, the upper shadow has bearish implications under certain conditions. These patterns, to have bearish implications, must in fact be after a rather pronounced up trend. The upper shadow means that the attempts of further highs made by buyers have given way to the return of sellers who have rejected the quotations, creating a rather important upper shadow. Therefore, we will be able to identify an area of resistance near the highs of this pattern. The pattern also indicates weakness for the immediately following session.

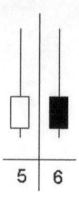

5 | 6

7. and 8. Lower shadow lines

Bullish implications. This candlestick pattern is specular to the previous one and to take on meaning it must form after a rather pronounced down trend. In this case, the further attempt at a bearish extension has found a return of buyers who have raised prices. In this case, we will be able to identify a support zone near the lows of the candle. This pattern generates a bullish expectation also for the following session. In these configurations, as well as in those of pattern 4, the color of the real body is of secondary importance, while the formation of a very pronounced 'shadow' is what matters.

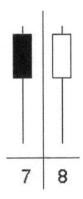

7 | 8

9. Doji, a situation of absolute balance

The absence of the real body (open = close) is an expression of maximum balance between buyers and sellers and therefore of market uncertainty. According to Japanese literature, the doji identifies that the 'market is at a crossroads'. The formation of a doji after periods of strong market direction is very significant. Very often the direction of the market for the following sessions is signaled by the breaking of the maximum (uptrend) or the low of the doji (downtrend).

9

Chapter 4 - Candlestick Patterns - Shooting Star

Now that we have seen what the main types of Japanese candlesticks are, let's examine from an operational point of view what the most important patterns that we can use to build our strategy with Japanese candlesticks are . Here are which ones we will cover in this chapter.

- Shooting Star
- Evening Star
- Hammer
- Inverted Hammer
- Hanging Man
- Engulfing
- Harami
- Doji
- Piercing Line and Dark Cloud Clover
- Tweezers Top and Tweezer Bottom
- Morning Star
- Homing Pigeon
- Descending Hawk

Shooting Star

Let's start with the first pattern, the shooting star. It is a typical candlestick pattern that finds its physiological location in an uptrend.

The pattern is composed of a small real body (candle body) and a long shadow in the upper part, while it is almost devoid of the shadow in the lower part.

Let's see what this candlestick pattern looks like graphically.

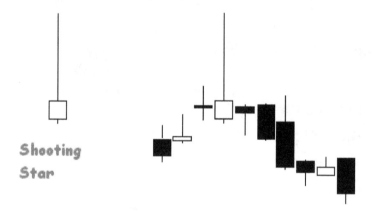

Shooting
Star

The textbook shooting star is the one that presents a gap compared to the candle that precedes it but, in many years of trading, we have noticed that even in the absence of the gap, the pattern remains reliable.

In intraday trading, it is also very rare to see the formation of a gap between one candle and the next, so it is necessary, so to speak, to 'settle down' and accept the pattern even in the absence of the gap.

The shooting star is a typical reversal pattern. In fact, the upper shadow means that buyers, in an uptrend, have tried to drive the market even higher but, at the end of the session, they have been overwhelmed by sellers who have rejected them.

The break of the minimum of the shooting star provides confirmation that the previous uptrend has lost strength and conviction and it offers us an excellent opportunity to take advantage of the imminent and probable decline.

Often the pattern appears straddling important resistances and in these cases it is even more significant. In fact, the upper shadow pierces the resistance by carrying out what in the jargon is called a 'breakout', but the bears then manage to bring the market back below that level.

The following example illustrates a couple of cases in which the Japanese shooting star candle performs its function as an inversion pattern very well.

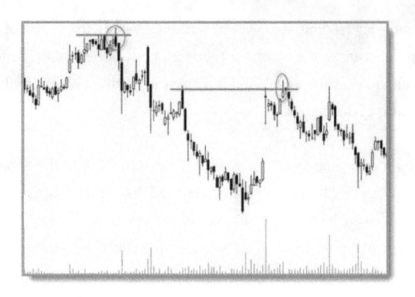

As you can see, in both cases the shooting star is formed close to resistance levels, first making the bullish breakout of the previous highs and then closing below the level broken on the upside shortly before.

The use normally made of this pattern is therefore to capture trend reversals, positioning short on the break of the minimum of the candlestick pattern.

An alternative use of the shooting star
There is a different way to use this pattern, which perhaps few people know.

On the one hand, in fact, the break of the minimum of the shooting star could give rise to a trend reversal, transforming the previous bullish trend into a bearish one, or in any case stopping it for a certain time.

On the other hand, the breakout of the high of the 'shooting star' pattern is even more significant, and often marks the continuation of the previously existing uptrend.

In fact, if the buyers, after having been won in the previous battle, manage again to bring the market back up above the maximum of the candle, a new flow of purchases will take place.

On the one hand, we have those who, finding confidence in the current trend, enter the market from scratch. On the other hand, there are also those operators who, taking advantage of the shooting star, had opened short positions and must now close the position at a loss, buying back the position sold, to avoid greater damage.

In the following example, we initially witness the formation of a shooting star, right next to an important level of resistance that portends an imminent reversal of the trend.

However, the shooting star in this case does not give rise to the expected reversal of the trend and, when the maximum of the pattern is exceeded, there is a strong acceleration of the upward trend already in place, as we can see in the following picture.

It seems quite evident that the shooting star can be used both in the traditional way as a reversal pattern, and in the less conventional way that we have just described, as a continuation pattern of the current uptrend.

This is an operational suggestion that can be exploited in all those cases of strong uptrend where the false signals of an imminent downside often follow one another without interruption.

Chapter 5 - Evening Start

This pattern in the candlestick graphical analysis is part of the three candlestick reversal and is a bearish pattern that develops in an uptrend.

The first candle is represented by a wide range white candle followed by a Star.

The central candle (the star, in fact) records a gap up with respect to the body of the previous candle, which we said must be wide-range and bullish, therefore with the closing greater than the opening.

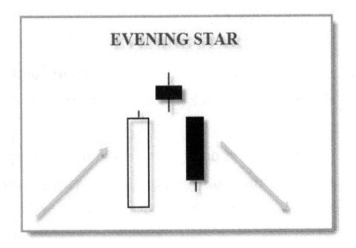

EVENING STAR

It is important to underline that the gap up must occur with respect to the body of the previous candle and not necessarily with respect to the maximum of the same.

The reduced size of the body of the central candle offers the first sign of indecision by traders about the continuation of the current trend.

The third candle records a gap down (negative) closing at an even lower level and thus completing the pattern.

In practice, the first broad-range candle confirms the uptrend, highlighting strong pressure from buyers. When the second candle (the star) makes a gap up, there is still residual bullish pressure on the market, eased immediately afterwards with the formation of a short range candle, which indicates indecision and possible trend reversal.

The body of this central candle can be indifferently white (positive close> open) or black (negative close <open).

If the central candle is a doji (i.e. a candle in which open and close coincide) the probability of reversal increases considerably, given the greater indecision present in the traders.

The third candle, clearly bearish, then confirms the reversal of the trend.

The evening star should have two gaps, one between the body of the first and that of the second candle and the other between the body of the second and that of the third candle, but personal experience leads us to affirm that we can rely on this pattern even in the absence of the second gap.

Moreover, in the intraday chart, it is really difficult for gaps to occur between one candle and the next, if not in the presence of news or significant macroeconomic data.

We can also verify in which graphic context the pattern is placed, in order to increase the probability of success of a trade that is based on this particular candlestick pattern.

Patterns of this type, which develop close to important resistances, in fact acquire even more significance.

As we see in the following chart, Bitcoin, already coming from a marked uptrend, recently made a broad-range bullish candle.

In the following session, prices opened with a gap up but immediately began to correct, creating a candle that in itself denotes strong negativity (close <open).

Let's see the graph

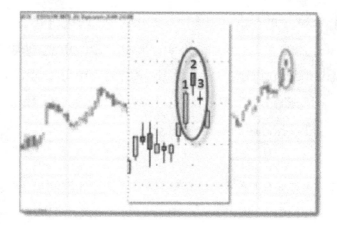

The opening of the third candle, which occurred below the star's minimum, confirms the potential inversion of the current trend. The following day, in fact, the stock opens with a strong gap down, even if we then notice an attempt to recover prices.

Finally, by tightening our graph again, we can verify that the pattern took place in a particular context, close to a static resistance.

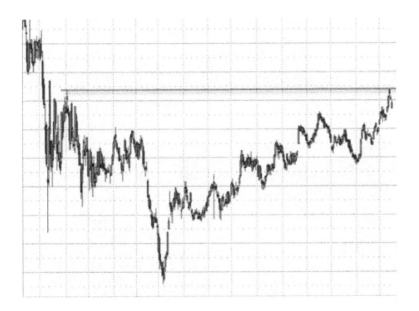

In short, in a case like this, the evening star formed just behind an important resistance zone increases the probability of success of the operation.

And so it was: the evening star, properly filtered, offered us a good trading opportunity with a low risk profile. We made a huge amount of money that day.

Chapter 6 - Hammer

The hammer is a reversal pattern of the bearish trend of candlestick analysis, consisting of a single candle. It is one of the patterns that do not need to be confirmed by subsequent candles, except for some special cases.

It is an easily identifiable pattern by the presence of a very small body and a long shadow that must be at least double the length of the body. This pattern is identifiable after a downtrend (a bearish trend) and often heralds an imminent market reversal. In fact, it identifies a price area in which buyers begin to face and resist sellers until they take over.

The color of the pattern is not very relevant, but a white body (close greater than open) has a slightly more bullish significance than the black body. A subsequent strongly bullish session confirms the reversal of the trend.

On the other hand, from the pattern it is not possible to obtain any indication on the duration of the inversion, which can be extrapolated only by looking at the general context.

Here's what the pattern looks like.

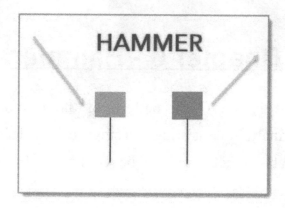

Let's summarize the conditions that allow you to classify the pattern as a 'hammer'.

- The shadow must be at least double than the body;
- The body must be at the top of the shadow. The color of the candle is not relevant but a positive body reveals a more bullish trend;
- The ideal pattern has no upper shadow which, if present, must still be small in size;
- A subsequent very positive candle definitively confirms the pattern.

Furthermore, here there are certain signals that can actually strengthen the reversal.

- The formation of the pattern in the proximity of support areas;
- The presence of a gap up in the next candle;

53

- A strong increase in volume during the formation of the hammer;
- The longer the shadow the greater the inversion signal;

If the downtrend continues, it is a sign that the bears are in control of the situation, but at some point, evidently because prices are deemed to be excessively 'discounted', massive purchases will begin to occur that will push the price towards the top of the range.

The return of purchases helps to create a small body and a very pronounced shadow.
This situation indicates that the bears are unable to maintain control of the market. In fact, as prices move above the hammer high in the next session, we have a strong indication that the bulls have taken over.

A positive session immediately following the formation of the hammer finally gives us the definitive confirmation of the reversal of the trend.

Let's see a first example on the Bitcoin daily chart, where the hammer formation triggered an abrupt and prolonged reversal of the trend.

Many traders, just to avoid staying out of the trade, anticipate the entry and enter into the purchase just as the lower shadows are being formed. Obviously, the potential downside is that the following day there will be a gap down opening and that the bearish trend continues completely displacing the buyers.

In this case the hammer accurately marks the end of the bearish trend and, after a first hesitation, in the following days the trend continues with a strong acceleration.

In conclusion, we can say that, as for other patterns, the larger the time frame used, the greater the reliability of the hammer. In fact, it must not be forgotten that the candlestick analysis was created for operations on a daily, if not weekly basis.

This does not mean that, as we have seen in the previous charts, the pattern cannot also be used for intraday trading, on hourly charts and even on 5-minute time frames.

In this case, an indicator such as the stochastic or the RSI, designed to highlight the oversold areas of the market (more on that in the next chapters), can be used as an additional filter for our hammer operation. Furthermore, a fun fact is that the hammer is perhaps the best known and most used pattern in candlestick trading.

Chapter 7 - Inverted Hammer

Let's continue the examination of candlestick patterns with another inversion pattern, probably one of the least known of the candlestick analysis: the inverted hammer.

Since this is a bullish reversal pattern we will find it after a bearish trend.

It is composed of a small body located on the lower part of the range and a long upper shadow which should have at least double the extension of the real body. In this case, the body color is not relevant.

In the classic pattern the lower shadow should not be present in any way, or in any case, it should be of little significance.

For this type of pattern it is prudent to wait for a confirmation that could be given by an opening of the next candle higher than the real body.

As with many other candlestick patterns, the rule is that the higher the time frame used, the higher the probability of success in the pattern. In any case, after entering to the upside, it is prudent to place a protective stop just below the low of the pattern.

Chapter 8 - Hanging Man

The hanging man is a candlestick pattern with bearish implications and is exactly the mirror image of the hammer analyzed above. We can find this pattern after a prolonged uptrend or, as we will see, even after a correction phase.

Unlike the hammer, the hanging man has a significantly higher probability of success, at least according to the statistics reported by experts. In our practice, it has been a pattern we have traded with a lot of success.

In fact, this pattern would have a 69% chance of success, compared to 41% of its opposite. Moreover, its recurrence, although quite frequent, is far less than that of the hammer. We see in the following picture how the pattern is formed.

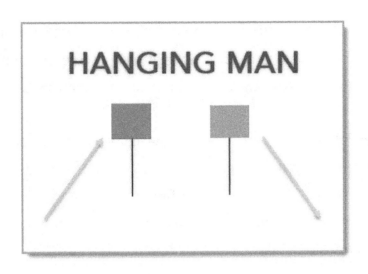

Psychological aspects of the hanging man

After a well-defined uptrend, the price still opens higher, but then begins to correct. The bears take control by pushing prices down, but before the candle closes, the bulls are once again able to bring the price back up, almost to the opening level.

To a careless observer, it might seem that the bulls still have control of the situation, but the long lower shadow shows that the bears have begun to position themselves at these levels, sounding a first alarm bell about the solidity of the bullish trend.

A strong downward movement in the following session would confirm that the bears have regained the upper hand, decreeing a trend reversal.

This is the reason why, before entering the position, we prefer to wait for the confirmation of the pattern in the immediately following candle with the break of the hanging man's low.

On the other hand, we consider the color of the body to be indifferent and so is the respect for the proportions (1: 3) between body and shadow. Even the presence of a small upper shadow does not affect the goodness of the pattern; indeed, it is quite frequent.

Let's now see some examples taken from real markets.

In the following chart we see the prices move in an uptrend making a top with a strong expansion candle (1), which is then followed by a pause (2) and then subsequently signing a gap up opening (indicated by the blue arrow).

The price begins to fall, a clear sign that the bears have taken over.

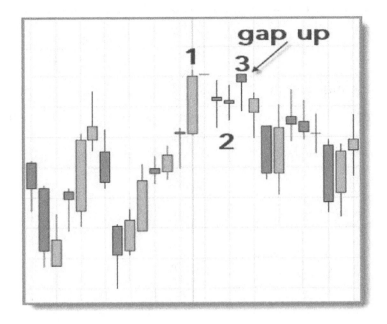

At some point, however, the bulls return and bring prices back up, thus creating the hanging man pattern (3).

In the following session, however, the price opens lower than the close of the previous candle and is no longer able to return to the highs.

The violation of the minimum of the hanging man confirms the pattern and triggers a real inversion of the trend.

In conclusion, it is good to reiterate that from an operational point of view it is preferable to open a short position only when the minimum of the hanging man is violated, placing a protective stop above the maximum of the pattern as shown in the image above.

In these conditions, in fact, the pattern has shown to have a higher probability of success, regardless of the reference time frame.

Chapter 9 - Engulfing

The engulfing pattern consists of two consecutive candles with a body of opposite color. The body of the second candle completely encloses the body of the previous candle.

Let's immediately clarify a doubt about this particular pattern with Japanese candlesticks. In classic candlestick analysis when we talk about engulfing we must consider only the bodies and not the shadows.

For your trading we suggest you take into consideration only those patterns that will occur after the development of a well-defined trend, discarding those that materialize in the lateral phases and therefore devoid of direction.

The first candle of the engulfing pattern has a narrow range body, while the next one has a wide range body. This is because the movement of the second candle is much wider than the previous one, as it could reflect the possible exhaustion of the current trend.

The amplitude of the two candles that make up the pattern can have a certain value. In fact, the more the range of the first candle is restricted and the wider the range of the second, the more reliable the pattern is.

The formation of this pattern is quite frequent and has a success rate of around 45%.
Let's first look at the bearish version of engulfing which is perhaps among the most important of the whole analysis with Japanese candlesticks as regards the trend reversal patterns

Bearish Engulfing
Prices are in an uptrend. At a certain point, a positive candle is created with a reduced range and with few volumes, an indication of range contraction and therefore of market indecision.

Here is what the bearish engulfing pattern looks like, a prelude to the reversal of an uptrend.

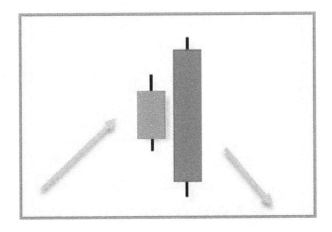

The next day the market opens above the previous high and collapses sharply with the close falling below the low of the previous candle.

Rising volumes on this second candle increase the reliability of the pattern.

This movement may lead us to think that the uptrend is beginning to falter; if the day following the completion of the pattern the prices settle at levels lower than the low of the second wide range candle, we have a confirmation that the current trend is no longer valid.

We are talking about days only because, as we have already mentioned, candlestick analysis and trading with Japanese candlesticks are born as a daily timeframe technique. However, it is still true that we can use all the patterns of this analysis also for intraday operations.

Obviously, the more we lower the time frame of our analysis, the more unreliable candlestick patterns will be.

Bullish Engulfing

The identification of the bullish Engulfing pattern is exactly the mirror image of the bearish one.

Let's see immediately what the bullish engulfing pattern looks like.

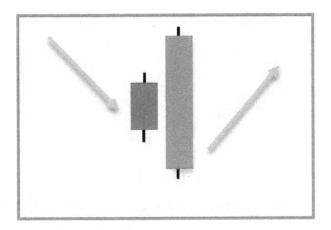

We are in the presence of a bearish trend, with the formation of a candle with a reduced range that goes in the same direction as the current trend. The next day, prices open below the previous day's low and begin to rise vigorously, closing above the previous day's opening.

If, after the completion of the pattern, prices remain above the maximum of the pattern, we have confirmation of the possible reversal of the trend.

Let's now see some examples taken from the real market.

In the picture below we have ETH with time frame daily.

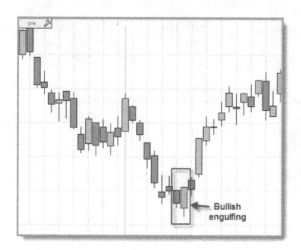

Bullish
engulfing

Prices are moving in a bearish trend. At a certain point, a candle with a negative body forms, in tune with the current trend, and the next day the prices open slightly below the previous day's low, fall a little further and then reverse the trend.

The prices then close on the highs of the day above the high of the previous day, forming the bullish engulfing candlestick pattern, which is a wide-range positive candle that completely incorporates the previous one.

In the following days, prices quote above the maximum of the pattern and then give rise to an uptrend that brings the cryptocurrency firmly to the upside. It is undoubtedly one of the most important candlestick patterns, perhaps the one that, in our experience, has the greatest chance of success.

Chapter 10 - Harami

It is a pattern whose formation is very frequent. In our personal experience we can say that, contrary to what we read in the various writings, it is a pattern with a relevance and reliability very similar to that of the engulfing pattern, if not even higher.

Let's see immediately how it is built and how to trade Japanese candlesticks with this pattern.

Bearish harami

The candles that make up the harami pattern are the same ones that also make up the engulfing pattern, but arranged inversely. In practice we have a two-candle formation, the second of which is 'inside'. This means it is entirely contained in the one that precedes it, within the limits which we will immediately discuss.

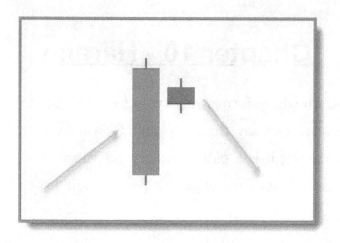

We find the bearish harami at the end of an uptrend or after an uptrend correction in a downtrend. It is formed by a wide range candle that totally encloses the candle that follows it, which must be in a narrow range.

In other words, it is only the body that must be enclosed in the previous candle, while the shadows have no value. From the most authoritative Japanese candlestick manuals we know that this pattern has a 50% success rate. However, even here the chances of success of the operation increase if we wait for a confirmation that occurs when prices violate the minimum of the pattern.

Let's see some examples on the real market.

Below is a daily chart of a cryptocurrency called Chainlink (ticker symbol: LINK). As we can see, the prices are coming from an uptrend.

Bearish Harami

Right on the top a strong positive expansion candle forms and in the following session, a narrow range negative inside candle appears on the chart. In the following sessions the price breaks the low of the pattern (green candle) and begins a descent that leads the cryptocurrency to lose more than 10% in a few sessions.

Bullish harami

As you can guess, the position of the candles is reversed with respect to that of the bearish harami.

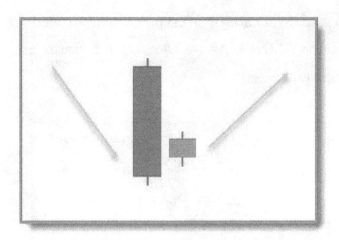

We have a wide range candle that totally encompasses the body of the candle that follows it which is a positive narrow range candle. We can find this formation at the end of a descending trend or after a bearish correction in an ascending trend.

The success rate of this pattern is always 50% (these are average values taken from the various specialist manuals) and as already mentioned, it is advisable to wait for confirmation in the days following its formation.

In the following chart we have an exceptional example of how these patterns can be used as a timing tool both to capture a trend reversal and to identify the continuation of the current trend.

As we see, in the chart below, the cryptocurrency (DOT in this case) is in a strong downtrend.

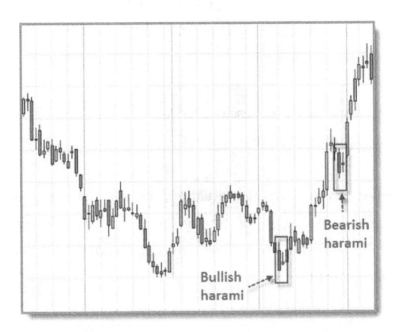

The prices, after having formed a first low, correct themselves and go down again. Apparently, the price has started to drop dramatically, forming wide range candles and with the last negative candle (first blue box) it almost touches the previous low (possible double bottom as we will see in the next chapters).

The next day, we have the formation of a noticeably narrow body inside the candle. This is what triggers the harami pattern.

In the following session, prices confirm the pattern, breaking the high and creating a sizable uptrend. Towards the middle of the movement, prices make a correction of just two candles (second blue box). After the second broad-range bearish candle we again have the formation of an inside daily candle. This is a candle with a significantly reduced body entirely contained in the one that precedes it.

Starting from the next session, prices explode upwards again with an expansion candle.

As we see in this particular situation, this pattern has given us an excellent indication of timing, accurately identifying the inversion of the trend and then signaling its continuation after the brief correction.

Chapter 11 - Doji

There are some types of Japanese candlesticks that are often able to identify major market turning points.

One of these patterns is undoubtedly the Doji.

On daily charts, Doji often indicate the beginning of a minor or intermediate trend, so recognizing this type of pattern can avoid common mistakes such as entering the market highs upwards or downwards on the lows. Or on the contrary it can provide us valid indications to take a position on the beginning of an important trend reversal.

There are 4 types of Doji candles. The classic Doji pattern has coincident closing and opening and a fairly narrow range and indicates considerable indecision.

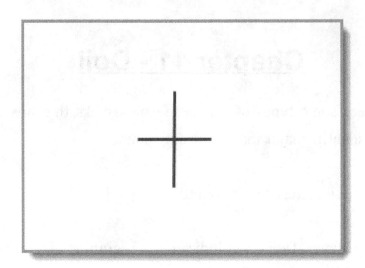

The second version is called the long-legged Doji, and it is always characterized by a coinciding opening and closing. However, it has a considerably wider range than the classic Doji.

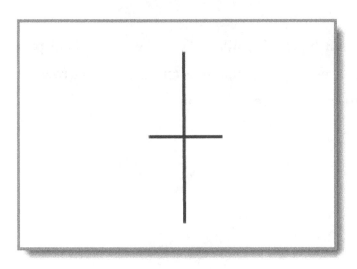

This pattern indicates a marked upward run in prices, then pushed back down to the opening level by strong profit taking. This kind of behavior of the operators, which are graphically returned by our candlestick pattern, indicates extreme indecision.

The third type of Doji is the Gravestone Doji, a candle with coincident opening and closing and a long upper tail. The name from its implications.

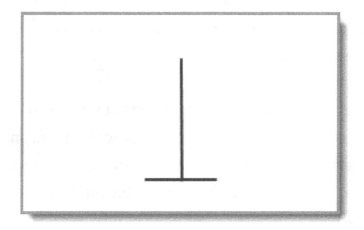

Also in this case we have a significant rise in prices that are strongly pushed down, up to the opening price by taking profits.

The latest version of this type of pattern is the Drangonfly Doji which is the opposite version of the Gravestone Doji.

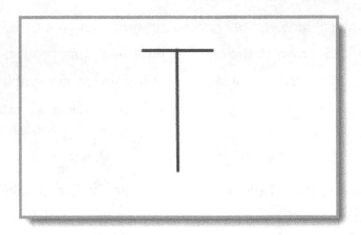

In this case, we have a sharp fall in prices, immediately after the opening, and then significant profit taking that pushes the price back to the opening level.

Operationally these last two patterns are not very usable. In fact, at least in our experience, being the shadow very pronounced, it is very 'expensive' to place the stop below the pattern (in the case of a bullish operation) or above (in the case of bearish operation).

Everything you need to know about the Doji

When a Doji pattern occurs we need to pay close attention to its position. If, for example, the Doji line occurs at the beginning of a trend, the chances that it will reverse the current trend are low.

Of course, we must not base our decision-making process only on a single Doji, but observe the graph as a whole to obtain more operational indications and further confirmations.

Therefore, the occurrence of a Doji near supports or resistances, or at the trendline test or still in support of price channels, can be a further confirmation of the significance of the pattern.

It is also important to wait for the candle following the Doji to confirm the validity of the pattern.

Below is a picture with some real examples from the Uniswap (ticker: UNI) price action.

Let's see how in the first case the Doji perfectly marks the exhaustion of the correction and the resumption of the current bearish trend.

In the second case we have the same condition, even if the development of prices has been a bit more troubled, the Doji has anticipated the indecision of the market and the restart of the primary trend. In the third case, a long Doji indicates the exhaustion of the movement in progress, anticipating the possible reversal of the trend.

The operation to be adopted with this pattern is extremely simple. You can enter a few ticks above the high of the figure in case of bullish trades, with stops below the low of the pattern. Or you can place the short order below the Doji minimum if the pattern indicates the imminent start of a bearish trend, with a stop above the maximum of the pattern.

Chapter 12 - Piercing Line and Dark Cloud Clover

The Piercing Line pattern is a two candlestick reversal pattern that forms after a downtrend or at the end of a correction in an uptrend. The first candle is black (i.e. negative) confirming the negative trend, while the second, which opens on a new low (gap), is white and closes above half of the previous candle.

The probability of success of this pattern is 47%. Therefore, it is advisable to wait for a confirmation, which can be given as always by the breaking of the maximum of the reversal candle (the positive one, in the example below).

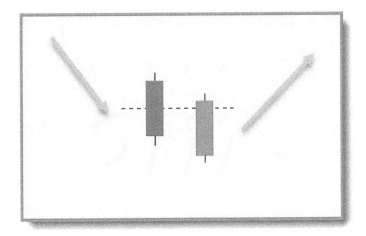

Let's see an example on the real market.

The following is the daily chart of XRP. As we can see, in the first part the price comes from a clearly negative trend.

Piercing line

On the lows of the trend, at the peak of the descent, after yet another strongly negative day, prices open in a gap down, momentarily continue their descent and then begin to rise.

Those who went short in the morning, or the day before in the wake of the strong wave of sales, when the price starts to rise again, is forced to close the bearish positions by buying the cryptocurrency back on the market and this action pushes the price even higher. The signal we derive from this configuration is of potential inversion.

The Dark Cloud cover pattern represents the bearish and mirrored version of the Piercing Line.

It is a classic Japanese candlestick reversal figure.

We can see the formation of this pattern after a prolonged uptrend or at the end of a correction in a downtrend.

Its formation consists of a first candle with a wide range of white color (i.e. positive) and a second candle, of opposite color that opens above the high of the previous candle and closes below its half.

The chances of success of this pattern are 47%, just like its opposite.

We know well that it may seem strange to talk about the success rates of a pattern because there are perhaps too many variables related to the use of a particular pattern. But several authoritative manuals offer us these statistics, so it seems appropriate to report them, then leaving the relevant considerations to the end user.

Even with this pattern it is advisable to wait for a confirmation to enter the position.

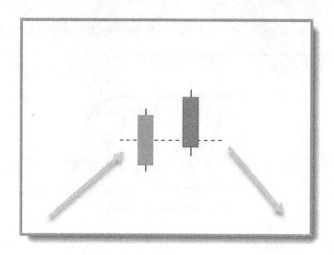

Also in this case, as in many other strategies with Japanese candlesticks, the reliability of the patterns increases if an indicator or oscillator is associated with the candlestick pattern that signals possible price divergences (Momentum, RSI, Stochastic etc) in correspondence with the occurrence of the pattern. As mentioned before, we will talk about indicators and oscillators in the next chapters.

Chapter 13 - Tweezer Top and Tweezer Bottom

This candlestick trading pattern consists of two candles with coincident highs or lows. This pattern is called 'tweezer' precisely because it is assimilated to the two ends of a tweezer.

In an uptrend a Tweezer pattern is formed when two highs coincide, conversely, in a downtrend it is formed when two lows coincide. The candles that form this pattern can take various shapes. They can have a more or less long body, the shadows of various sizes and even the presence of a Doji candle could contribute to the creation of a Tweezer pattern.

This pattern acquires more value when it occurs at the end of a strong bullish or bearish move and also when there is a reversal candle in its formation which can give rise to another two-candlestick pattern.

Let's see how the bearish version of this pattern is formed.

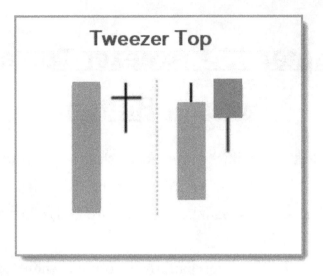

And this is the bullish version of the pattern.

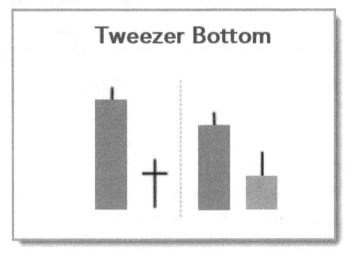

What we see in the two pictures are only a few possible examples of the pattern. The important thing is that the pattern respects the conditions described above. In essence, it is a question of identifying very close double highs or double lows.

In the absence of a reversal candle as the second candle, the pattern is very weak, especially if we find it on daily charts. On weekly or monthly charts, on the other hand, it has a higher value as it deals with double tops or bottoms quite distant in time.

Therefore, while on a daily level we prefer the formation of a second candle having the characteristics of a reversal in order to strengthen the pattern, on a weekly or monthly level we can also do without it.

Let's analyze some examples on charts taken from the real market.

The following is the daily chart of Litecoin (ticker: LTC).

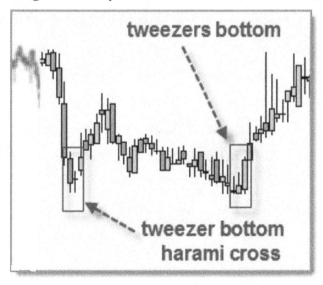

The price comes from a long descent that accelerates precisely in the final part. The downward movement is stopped by a Tweezer formation.

We note that the second candle of the formation is a Doji which, together with the previous candle, forms a Harami Cross, the bullish reversal pattern that we have already covered in this chapter.

Prices rise, try to descend again but stop once more at the same low with a further Tweezers formation, even with three candles, a sign that we are facing very strong support. The Tweezer bottom formation, reinforced by the previous Harami pattern, gives rise to a real trend reversal.

It is not uncommon to find this pattern on the low or high of the market and, as we see, if strengthened in its formation by a reversal candle, the pattern can be exploited with profit. As always, we enter above the maximum of the pattern with a stop below the minimum for bullish operations. Obviously, the contrary is true for short operations.

Chapter 14 - Morning Star

The Morning Star configuration is a bullish reversal candlestick pattern. Let's see what this pattern looks like.

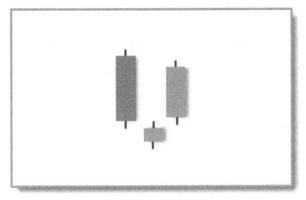

The pattern consists of a broad-range bearish candle, followed by a narrow-range candle which has a negative opening gap.

The third candle is represented by a bullish candle which, once again, has an opening gap, this time positive, relative to the narrow range candle.

Contrary to what one might think, the probability of success of this pattern does not exceed 50% (percentage detected by the statistics of Gregory Morris). Therefore, in our many years of trading experience we have devised some tricks aimed at avoiding some of the most frequent false signals generated by this interesting graphic configuration. Before moving on to some examples taken from the cryptocurrency market, we would like to clarify what might seem too obvious: when you go from theory to practice, or from candlestick manuals to the real market, finding the perfect pattern is not so frequent.

This is obviously a general argument that applies to any pattern conformation, even for those of classical technical analysis.

In the case of the Morning Star, the perfect pattern would foresee a gap both between the first and the second candle, and between the second and the third.

Chapter 15 - Homing Pigeon

Let's now see the first of two Japanese candlestick patterns that should already be familiar not only because they are often found in candlestick charts but also because they have a lot in common with the Harami, one of the patterns we have already covered in this chapter.

The patterns in question are the Homing Pigeon and the Descending Hawk.

These two patterns are the opposite of each other in terms of implications. The first is a bullish pattern and the second is a bearish pattern.

These are two candlestick patterns that closely resemble the Harami pattern, with the difference that while in the Harami we necessarily have opposite colors for the two candles that make up the pattern, these two patterns have the two candles of the same color.

Less experienced traders who are faced with these two particular patterns do not take them into consideration because they do not know their implications. However, they have the same validity and effectiveness as the Harami.

Let's see the bullish version, called the Homing Pigeon.

We find this pattern in a descending market and it is a pattern that, like its corresponding bearish Descending Hawk, highlights a weakening of the current trend until it often takes the form of a real reversal figure.

The Homing Pigeon is formed by a first broad-range bearish candle (close <open), followed by a candle included within the broad-range candle that precedes it, as shown in the image.

In the picture, the pattern is represented in its optimal configuration, the one that in traditional technical analysis corresponds to the so-called 'inside' candle.

Moreover, the Homing Pigeon differs from the traditional inside candle in that in this candlestick pattern only the body of the second candle must be included in the first candle, while it is not necessary that the shadows remain within the range of the previous candle.

The following is the daily chart of the cryptocurrency Monero (ticker: XMR).

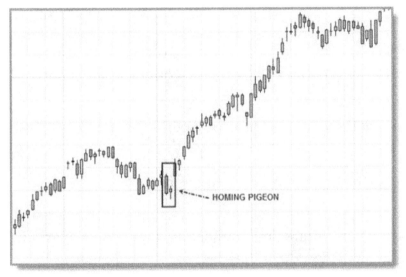

The position of this pattern in the chart is interesting because it is found after a correction of the dominant uptrend, therefore it provides the input to open a position suited to the underlying trend.

As we see, the prices come from an initial upward phase. At some point, the upside takes a break and the prices correct downwards.

At the very end of this correction we find our Homing Pigeon pattern. We have a broad-range negative first candle that would suggest a continuation of the downtrend. The next day the price opens within the wide range candle, breaks the previous day's low and then retrieves it and closes within the previous candle.

We reiterate, as already highlighted above, that in Japanese candlesticks the shadows are of less importance than the body. Well, this pattern is precisely an expression of this principle since to identify the Homing Pigeon we only consider the body.

Therefore the pattern is also verified in the case highlighted in the graph where the shadow of our Homing Pigeon comes out of the range of the candle that precedes it.

This pattern occurs less frequently than its similar bullish Harami, but has a slightly higher probability of success, according to the statistics offered by G. Morris.

As always, before entering a trade it is advisable to wait for the confirmation of the pattern that occurs with the bullish break of the broad range candle that completes the setup of the pattern.

Chapter 16 - Descending Hawk

Above we have just dealt with the bullish version of this pattern. Now instead we will illustrate the bearish version which has a similar structure but opposite colors.

The pattern in question is the Descending Hawk.

This pattern, with a funny denomination like many other candlestick patterns, is formed by a positive (close> open) wide range candle followed by a candle, always positive, with a smaller range than the first.

As a result, we have a day in which the trend was largely positive followed by a day in which prices, despite having always had a positive action, remained within the previous candle.

We can see the structure of the pattern in the following picture.

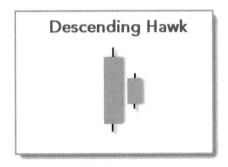

Descending Hawk

Chapter 17 - How to study Japanese Candlesticks Patterns

As we have seen in the previous chapters, the trading strategy with Japanese candlesticks is certainly one of the most effective approaches for those who are starting to approach the financial markets.

Studying Japanese candlesticks, the mechanisms underlying their formation, and the individual candlestick patterns, is the best way to fully understand the mechanisms behind the formation of prices and the movements of the cryptocurrency market.

The advice we can give, in fact, beyond learning the individual patterns 'by heart', is to learn to understand with a single glance what is happening on the market simply by observing the shape of the candlesticks, individually and in their context.

A long lower tail (shadow), formed close to a support after a prolonged drop in prices, must immediately make you understand that the buyers are back in strength by recovering the ground lost previously.

Therefore, beyond remembering that this pattern has the name of 'Hammer', it is important to understand the mechanisms underlying the formation of candlestick patterns in order to be immediately reactive and operational. The terms of any trading strategy with Japanese candlesticks and single patterns, at least the most recurring ones, can be learned quite quickly.

From an operational point of view, to apply candlestick patterns to your trading, it is important to follow the advice in the previous chapters which, basically, can be summarized as follows.

- **Always wait for a confirmation before getting into a position.** The confirmation can be given by the breaking of the low of the pattern if it is a bearish candlestick pattern or, vice versa, the breaking of the maximum if you are dealing with a bullish pattern.

- **Filter the signals that derive from the analysis with Japanese candlesticks through an oscillator or indicator.** We will talk more about these two topics in the next chapters, just trust us on this point for now.

- **Always remember to place a stop loss.** This is an order to protect your capital if the operation does not go in the desired direction. The stop loss must normally be positioned above the maximum of the pattern in the case of bearish operations or below the minimum of the pattern if the operation is bullish.

Finally a piece of advice that applies to every type of trading is to use leverage appropriate to your risk profile and if the stop loss during the opening of the position turns out to be too large, move on. There will certainly be many other occasions.

Conclusion

Congratulations on making it to the end of this book, we hope you found some useful insights to take your cryptocurrency trading skills to the next level. As you should know by now, the world of cryptocurrency is extremely complicated and there is a new "opportunity" every way you look. However, our experience tells us that only by taking things seriously and having a proper plan you can develop your trading skills to the point that you can trade for a living.

Our final advice is to stay away from the shining objects that the world of cryptocurrencies offers you every day. Choose a cryptocurrency you want to master and study it in depth. After you have a sufficient knowledge on what you are talking about, apply the fundamental and technical analysis strategies we have discussed in this book. Analyze your results, improve your money management skills and become the master of your emotions.

As you can see, there are no shortcuts you can take. Easy money does not exist. What exists is the possibility to start from zero and work your way up to become a professional trader. The journey might be difficult, but it is certainly worth it.

Bitcoin Trading

Discover the Futures, Options and DCA Trading and Investing Strategies to Build Wealth During the 2021 Bull Run – Cryptocurrency and Blockchain Secrets Unveiled!

damages that may befall them after undertaking information described herein.

Additionally, the information in the following pages is intended only for informational purposes and should thus be thought of as universal. As befitting its nature, it is presented without assurance regarding its prolonged validity or interim quality. Trademarks that are mentioned are done without written consent and can in no way be considered an endorsement from the trademark holder.

Introduction

Bitcoin has taken the world by storm once again when it crossed $20,000 per BTC in December of last year. After more than 2 years of bear market, the most famous cryptocurrency surpassed its previous all time high.

A lot of people are now trying to improvise themselves as professional investors and are losing a lot of money, only helping those who actually know what they are doing accumulate an incredible amount of wealth that will lead to generational fortunes.

To join the club of the few investors that actually make it, you need the right strategies and the right mindset. Notice how we did not include a large initial capital. In fact, while having more money to trade with means having more fire power, it is not necessary to have thousands of dollars to accumulate Bitcoin and build wealth.

In fact, when we started investing in Bitcoin we only had a few hundreds to put into the market, but that sum yielded us thousands and thousands of dollars over the span of a few years.

In this book you are going to discover all the strategies that have allowed us to take investing skills to the next level and

111

everything that helped us understand Bitcoin. If you diligently apply our advice, we are sure you are going to see amazing results in a relative short period of time, since this bull run is offering an amazing number of opportunities.

Please, stay away from all the shiny objects of the cryptocurrency world. Just focus on Bitcoin, study it deeply and then milk it like a cash cow!

To your success!

Charles Swing and *Masaru Nakamoto*

Chapter 1 - Legal framework

The legal nature of bitcoin is not a uniformly decided issue. The international aspect of bitcoin, with regard to the regional nature of the legal frameworks (European Union, United States, China, in particular), precludes any comprehensive legal response, in the current state of the law.

In particular, the G20 considered that if crypto assets raise issues with regards to consumer and investor protection, market integrity, tax evasion, money laundering and terrorist financing, then they must be managed by states rather than by the G20 itself.

European Union

According to the European Central Bank, the important banking and financial regulations imposed on the Member States of the European Union do not concern bitcoin. The European banking authority warned consumers against the risks associated with bitcoin (December 13th, 2013), considering cryptocurrencies as "virtual representations" of money. It also recommended on

July 4th, 2014 to European banking and financial institutions not to use bitcoin nor to offer services around it.

On October 22nd, 2015, the Court of Justice of the European Union confirmed that bitcoin exchange transactions for traditional currencies were exempt from VAT, considering bitcoin as a "virtual currency" and not as a good or a service.

Australia

In December 2013, the Governor of the Central Bank of Australia (RBA) said in an interview on the legality of bitcoin that "there would be nothing to stop people from deciding to transact in another currency in a store if they wanted. There is no law against this, so we have competing currencies".

Australia has officially confirmed that bitcoin will be treated as cash on July 1st, 2017 and that it will no longer be subject to double taxation.

Belgium

The Minister of Finance indicated that government intervention with regard to the Bitcoin system does not appear to be necessary, since it is the European Union that should be focused on regulating this subject.

The central bank of Belgium estimated in a statement that "the threats to monetary stability posed by digital currencies issued by private actors are currently rather limited, because they used as a medium of exchange, so that their impact on the conditions in the economy is weak".

China

On December 5th, 2013, the Chinese Central Bank banned local banks from any bitcoin transaction, a measure leading to the start of a crash in the value of the virtual currency. BTC China, the world's leading bitcoin transaction platform, prohibited users from making new deposits in Yuan into their account "following new government regulations". On January 8th, 2014, the Chinese group Ali Baba banned bitcoin payments, in accordance with new Chinese regulations. A law established on September 4th, 2017 leads either to the closure of an exchange platform or to the end of the acceptance of fiat currencies. In February 2018, the Chinese government announced that it wanted to strengthen the ban through censorship of all Chinese or foreign bitcoin exchange websites.

South Korea

In South Korea bitcoin and cryptocurrencies are legal and recognized as financial instruments.

There are no restrictions for holding and exchanging bitcoin between individuals. Exchange platforms must ensure they have at least 500 million Korean Won to protect traders and businesses from embezzlement and fraud.

The government of South Korea has agreements with 14 "virtual cash" exchange platforms known as currency exchanges. Thanks to these agreements, these platforms only accept users whose identity is controlled by a financial actor such as a bank.

United States

The parliamentary report by Senator Tom Carper (February 3rd, 2014) provided a first overview of the legal issues of bitcoin.

The report concluded on the economic interest of bitcoin and the need to regulate its development, in order to contain its specific risks. It also did not offer a firm legal definition of bitcoin.

On February 26th, 2014, US Senator Joe Manchin called for bitcoin to be banned in the United States, because of its uncontrolled volatility and the risk that it could be used for illegal purposes, in particular for money laundering. For the moment, the United States considered that virtual currencies developed on the bitcoin model have no legal value but constitute assets liable to be subject to taxes.

On December 10th, 2017, the Chicago Stock Exchange institutionalized Bitcoin, launching the possibility to trade Bitcoin futures.

In 2018, the authorities - notably the Securities and Exchange Commission, and the Commodity Futures Trading Commission - prosecuted various actors who carried out scams such as the dangling of the possibility of getting rich with Bitcoin or binary options.

France

In France, neither the law nor case law has specifically and clearly regulated the nature and legal regime of bitcoin. For some lawyers, it is not a currency. For others, bitcoin would be "a currency, electronic in nature, devoid of legal tender". For the national commission of campaign accounts and political financing, it is a "currency without defined legal status". For the Directorate General of Public Finances, bitcoin is considered to be a movable property, the value at purchase or sale and its value at the end of the fiscal year being legal.

In the event that Bitcoin is considered to be electronic money, the rules in force for electronic money would apply to bitcoin (Articles L. 133-29 et seq. 191 of the Monetary and Financial Code). In other cases, a legal regime for Bitcoin would have to be invented.

In a 2014 report it was stated that virtual currency did not represent a claim on the issuer and was not issued against the remittance of funds, within the meaning of the electronic money directive, which did not give it the electronic money status. On the other hand, no text excludes bitcoin transactions from the tax obligations in force, in particular with regard to the taxation of profits or the collection of capital gain tax. This situation was recalled by the tax authorities on July 11th, 2014. Similarly, profits made in accordance with the definition of article 92 of the General Tax Code (CGI) are subject to taxation.

In January 2018, the Minister of the Economy, Bruno Le Maire, said he understood "the risks of speculation and possible embezzlement". He entrusted a mission on bitcoin to Jean-Pierre Landau, former deputy governor of the Banque de

France. In his report, Jean-Pierre Landau recommends not directly regulating crypto-currencies (except in the context of the fight against money laundering), to create an environment favorable to the development of this technology and to strictly limit the exposure of the financial sector to cryptocurrencies. On September 12th, 2018, France became the first country in the world to grant a legal framework to Initial Coin Offerings.

Japan

The central bank of Japan officially recognizes bitcoin and cryptocurrencies as a means of payment. In fact, article 2-5 of the amended PSA specifies that virtual currencies are accepted as a means of payment without being legal currencies.

United Kingdom

Bitcoin is considered "private money". When cryptocurrencies are exchanged for pounds sterling or other fiat currencies, such as the euro or the dollar, no VAT is due. However, VAT applies for all goods and services that could be exchanged for bitcoins. Profits and losses made on cryptocurrencies are subject to capital gains tax.

Russia

On February 6th, 2014, Russia declared the currency illegal on its territory, arguing that the only official currency in Russia is the ruble and that no other currency can legally be used in the country.

Singapore

In December 2013, the Singapore Monetary Authority asserted that trading in goods and services for bitcoins constituted trade in which it was not for the authority to intervene.

In January 2014, Singapore's Domestic Revenue Administration released a set of tax guidelines according to which bitcoin transactions can be considered barter if they are used as a method of payment for real goods and services. Companies that deal in bitcoin exchanges will be taxed based on their sales levels.

Swiss

In Switzerland, the Federal Council considered that bitcoin is a virtual currency of marginal use, and that as such it is subject in principle to the legislation of regular currencies. However, it recommends that authorities and responsible consumer organizations call on bitcoin users to be cautious.

According to the Federal Council, the execution of contracts concluded in virtual currencies can in principle be ensured and offenses committed with these currencies are punishable.

For example, the professional trading of virtual currencies and the operation of trading platforms in Switzerland fall in principle within the scope of the law on money laundering, which requires the identity of the person to be verified.

However, from the Swiss point of view, there are no international standards regulating virtual currencies.

Bitcoin will always exist, whether prohibited or advised by the authorities, you just need to connect to the internet by cable or satellite to make a transaction in your ledger. In addition, people residing in countries hostile to bitcoin can use a method such as those proposed by Samourai or Wasabi, for example, to avoid being traced.

The debate around Bitcoin and terrorism

Various opinions relating to the real or supposed link between Bitcoin and terrorism have been raised.

On several occasions, Bitcoin has been touted as a tool that can be used for terrorist financing their criminal actions. In our opinion, stating that Bitcoin can be used for terrorism is as saying that dollars can be used for the same reason. Both statements could be true, but we will never consider stopping using dollars because of this potential issue.

Chapter 2 - Potential Risks Linked to the Bitcoin Network

From the outset, Bitcoin has been the subject of many discussions, both technical and economic, and even political.

From these discussions, a number of advantages and disadvantages of the Bitcoin network were discussed. Some of these comments are not necessarily specific to bitcoin and could be applied to other payment systems with similar characteristics.

However, recently, we realized that the risks associated with bitcoin are little or poorly understood in their nature and extent.

Bitcoin, like most existing cryptocurrencies, has no underlying assets or collateral. Whoever buys a bitcoin exclusively pays the seller. Therefore, the increase in the value of money comes exclusively from the continued presence of a flow of buyers able to support its price. Therefore, on closer inspection, the functioning of bitcoin might seem much more similar to that of a pyramid system than to that of a monetary system. However, if you have followed us so far, you know that in reality things are quite different. In fact, when you store bitcoins you contribute to the stability and strength of the monetary network, which

123

grows and strengthens itself from the amount of money that investors pour into it.

Volatility

Bitcoin is a volatile currency because the number of coins is limited in the face of growing demand. The price evolves according to the news on crypto-currencies. Cryptocurrency is floating like any currency and fluctuates differently against different currencies.

Irreversibility

A bitcoin transaction is irreversible and cannot be reversed. This means that if you give or type the wrong address, you will have lost your coins for good.

Depending on the internet

The Bitcoin protocol is an overlay of the IP protocol which is the basis of the functioning of the internet. In the event of an internet shutdown (massive power / IT failure or forced shutdown by a government of internet providers' routers, for example) or if a government does not promote or defend internet neutrality, the Bitcoin protocol could be slowed down or even completely blocked.

Technical limitations of the network

The size of the database has grown very rapidly and requires several gigabytes of memory in a hard drive. Some experts have questioned the future size of this database and are discussing possible solutions to save disk space such as pruning the oldest transactions that form the Merkle tree. However, this does not seem necessary given the progress made in storage technologies.

The size of the block is another important aspect. Bitcoin "super-nodes" are being considered to facilitate the propagation of information through the nodes of the network and which struggle to keep up with the increase in the size of the database. Some scholars argue that Moore's Law could help track network growth using personal computers.

Institutional risk

To convert cryptocurrency to currency it is often necessary to go through an exchange platform operated by private companies, which are potentially vulnerable to defaults or bankruptcies, as happened to Mt. Gox. However, it is possible to exchange your bitcoins for cash, gold or a service in order to avoid this pitfall.

Environmental impacts and risks

They are linked to the electricity consumption generated by mining, which represents, according to estimates, from 0.15% to 0.32% of the world electricity consumption. They are low when it is produced from renewable energies, but important for fossil fuels (global warming and air pollution). More and more server farms are installed in countries with cold climates (to facilitate their cooling) with cheap renewable energies, such as Canada and Iceland.

A study on the origin of the electricity consumed by mining farms shows that 74.1% of the energy consumed is produced from renewable energies. However, following criticism, the lead author of the study admitted there were some mistakes in the research. Indeed, the major renewable energy in China, hydroelectricity, is only available at low cost in certain periods of the year. The rest of the year electricity production comes mainly from coal.

Ethical risks

Bitcoin would favor the first acquirers of the currency ("early adopters"). This claim is sometimes confirmed by certain studies showing that the distribution of wealth in bitcoin is very unequal.

It has been suggested that Bitcoin could be likened to a Ponzi scheme, but this is not applicable as we have seen in the previous pages as well. In fact, the price of the cryptocurrency is a balance between buyers looking to acquire the currency and sellers looking to sell it. In a Ponzi scheme, new entrants pay early adopters and receive nothing in return.

Some central banks (ECB, Banque de France, Bank of China) have issued warnings on the use of bitcoin insisting on its highly speculative character, on the legal risks it generates due to its status as an unregulated currency and on its possible use for criminal purposes (money laundering, terrorist financing). The European Banking Authority (EBA) also issued a warning in December 2013 against the lack of consumer protection through the use of the payment method that is bitcoin. However, other institutions hold a more nuanced or even opposite approach. Thus, the German and American governments regard this currency with a certain benevolence and Ben Bernanke, ex-president of the FED, stated that bitcoin has potential to revolutionize the monetary system.

Chapter 3 - Mixed Opinions on Bitcoin

Economists have expressed various opinions on bitcoin. For the American Nobel Laureate in Economics Joseph Stiglitz, bitcoin is a bubble that will be very exciting as long as it goes up before it goes down. For him, it does not serve any socially useful function. Its success is due to its ability to circumvent. As a result, he feels that bitcoin should be banned for good.

The French Nobel laureate in economics Jean Tirole warns against bitcoin, stating that it is "an asset without intrinsic value", "without economic reality". He is dubious in terms of two criteria: is it a viable currency in the long term? Does it contribute to the common good? Regarding viability, Jean Tirole is particularly critical of the Initial coin offering (ICO) of three billion dollars in 2017. Advertised as an instrument of financial disintermediation, according to him ICOs neglect the fundamentals of finance. In fact, the use of reliable and well-capitalized intermediaries to monitor projects is fundamental to ensure everything is done correctly. For the economist, the social role of Bitcoin is "elusive". Bitcoins are concentrated in private hands, particularly for fraud and tax evasion.

Bill Gates (ex-CEO of Microsoft), Jack Dorsay (CEO of Twitter), Richard Branson, Chamath Palihapitiy (co-founder of Facebook), the Winklevoss brothers and a series of other billionaires see bitcoin as inevitable.

Jean-Marc Sylvestre, French journalist for the business press, predicts a crash by highlighting its success among those who make dirty money in the drug trade, the illicit guns trade and in international prostitution as well as among populations of emerging countries, who do not have a bank account but are equipped with a smartphone. To this can be added the key role of bitcoin in ransomware attacks, with ransomware often demanding payment in this currency, which is difficult to trace.

As you can see, there are different opinions on Bitcoin and its validity as a currency. Actually, we believe it to be more like digital gold, which is the same idea shared by Michael Saylor, CEO of Microstrategy, and Elon Musk.

In the next chapters we are going to discuss the technical aspects you need to know if you want to buy bitcoin and store it in a safe way.

Chapter 4 - Buying Bitcoin

The turnover regarding virtual currencies is constantly increasing, as evidenced by the interest of users on cryptocurrency exchanges. Even if Bitcoin is the best known worldwide, it does not mean that it is the only cryptocurrency to be bought or sold.

Choosing the best cryptocurrency exchange is essential, especially in consideration of the total invested capital value. In fact, there are risks associated with cryptocurrency investing, one of these refers precisely to the choice of the exchange.

Before listing the best exchange sites for buying and selling cryptocurrencies, we will explain in detail what an exchange is and how it works. Therefore, we will focus on the most advantageous solutions on the market today, available to experienced investors and users who are entering the digital currency sector only now.

Cryptocurrency exchanges

Cryptocurrency exchanges are platforms where coins can be exchanged. The most common exchange takes place between dollars or euros for the corresponding value of a virtual currency. For example, if you want to buy one BTC, you will need $58,000 (the present value of a single BTC) plus the commission value for the exchange.

Once the exchange is complete, the newly acquired cryptocurrency must be deposited in a wallet (electronic wallet). The wallet can be compared to a bank account, with which, however, one only has the opportunity to withdraw, deposit or send part or all of the cryptocurrency to another digital wallet or exchange.

The wallet

Each wallet is assigned a specific address, which could be compared to the bank account number code of traditional checking accounts. In addition, a secret key is needed to log into the electronic wallet for the first time. You can then set a login password and encrypt the data.

There are three types of wallets.

- **Software Wallet.** A program downloaded to a computer or mobile device. They are generally among the wallets that guarantee greater security.

- **Online Wallet.** Digital wallets that can be accessed from the Internet through a private key, most often managed by the exchange. Of the three types it is the least safe.

- **Hardware Wallet**. A physical device (most often a USB stick) that makes it possible to access the wallet only if it is connected to a second device. Among all it is the one that offers the greatest safety.

We will talk more about cryptocurrency wallets in a dedicated chapter.

As there are different wallets, there are also different types of exchanges.

- **Exchange fiat to crypto.** They allow you to exchange a fiat currency (e.g. dollar or euro) for a virtual currency.

- **Exchange with centralized management**. Platforms managed by a third party. The positive aspects include the speed of transactions and the low commissions compared to those requested by exchanges for decentralized cryptocurrencies. Among the disadvantages, however, there is a greater risk of running into a scam.

- **Exchange with decentralized management.** The processes are automated, as everything is delegated to the blockchain technology. Consequently, an exchange of this type operates in total safety. However, it is also true that transactions are slower. Furthermore, the variety of cryptocurrencies is still small compared to the offer of other exchanges.

The last aspect to emphasize concerns the commissions, charged to users who operate within the exchange platforms. Broadly speaking, there are four different fees.

- Storage fee;
- Withdrawal fee;
- Order taker fee;
- Order maker fee.

Usually, the fees are inversely proportional to the volumes traded on a monthly basis. This means that higher volumes correspond to lower fees, while when volumes are low, fees tend to rise.

Therefore, if we want to summarize the concepts expressed so far, the choice of an exchange rather than another should be based on the analysis of three important aspects.

- **Safety**. As far as possible, opting for a decentralized exchange platform would be the best decision, but it is also true that it is a rather recent solution with the limitations described above (low speed of operations and few cryptocurrencies to trade).

- **Strategy**. Before choosing an exchange instead of another, you should have already outlined a plan. In this regard, it is important to understand if you want to aim for a fiat-to-crypto exchange or an exchange where only virtual currencies exist.

- **Commissions**. An analysis of the costs to be incurred for the future operations that will be carried out is very important to make a final choice, taking into account the other two factors as well.

The best cryptocurrency exchanges

The list of the best cryptocurrency exchanges features long-lived platforms such as Coinbase Pro, Kraken and Bitstamp, in addition to the more modern Binance. Below we offer a brief presentation of each trading platform, listing pros and cons.

Binance

Binance is the largest international cryptocurrency exchange. Created only in 2017, in a short time it managed to gain the interest of virtual currency traders.

Binance has also recently created its own cryptocurrency (Binance Coin, ticker symbol: BNB). Currently BNB is in the top ten positions of the CoinmarketCap ranking, dominated by Bitcoin and Ethereum.

Until recently, traders on Binance could only trade cryptocurrencies with other cryptocurrencies. Recently, however, the possibility of exchanging virtual currencies in exchange for fiat currencies has also been introduced.

The main advantages are that there are over 130 cryptocurrencies available and the commissions are around 0.1%. The only disadvantage is that the graphic interface is not very beginner friendly. In fact, we found that people that are just starting out in cryptocurrency find it difficult to navigate through the many possibilities of the site. It is the Ferrari of cryptocurrency exchanges: if you want to buy bitcoin for the first time you do not need a Ferrari.

Wirex

Wirex is a digital payment platform, and an FCA-licensed electronic money institution in the United Kingdom, with a clear mission: to cancel the differences between real and virtual money and make the use of cryptocurrencies easier and more accessible to everyone.

Thanks to the innovative mobile app and the new generation Wirex multi-currency card, the user can buy, exchange and hold a wide range of fiat coins and cryptocurrencies (including BTC, ETH, LTC, XRP, XLM, WXT, WAVES, DAI and NANO) and also spend them in physical stores. All this quickly, safely and without commission. There are many advantages of having a Wirex account, from unlimited access to OTC rates for cryptocurrency exchanges, to new generation rewards.

Services offered and benefits

- **Currency exchange without commission**. Users can exchange fiat and cryptocurrencies instantly on the app for free and at favorable exchange rates.

- **Wirex multi-currency card.** This allows users to spend cryptocurrencies and fiat money wherever Mastercard and Visa are accepted, and participate in the first cryptocurrency cashback program in the world (Cryptoback) to get up to 2% of the cost for each purchase made.

- Free ATM withdrawals up to $500 per month and no monthly fee.

Among the advantages offered by Wirex there are also the free account setup and card issuance and the absence of commissions on card transactions in stores. Furthermore, users have the possibility of recharging the account without restrictions up to 50,000 dollars per transaction by bank transfer.

Sign up process and verification

To register, you need to connect to the website or download the app available for free on the App Store and Play Store. The registration procedure is quick and easy: just fill out the form and click on the link received in the confirmation email.

The verification process takes only a few minutes. You will have to upload the documents to verify your identity and, once verified, set a password for greater security. And speaking of security, to protect its users' data from possible hacker attacks and violation of privacy, Wirex uses SSL (Secure Sockets Layer) technology for all communications between servers and web browsers, which guarantees data protection. Furthermore, two-factor authentication and BitGo's multi-signature technology, which makes it impossible to transfer money without the transaction being authorized with signature by all parties involved. Finally, the platform does not keep payment card numbers, expiration dates or CVV codes. It is a very nice app for buying your first bitcoin, we recommend it.

Coinbase Pro

Coinbase Pro is the world's best known cryptocurrency exchange. It is based in San Francisco and also appears in the ranking of the longest-lived platforms (the year of Coinbase's foundation dates back to 2012).

Compared to other exchanges, there are few cryptocurrencies available for trading in Coinbase Pro. The updated list features Bitcoin, Bitcoin Cash, Ethereum, Litecoin, EOS, Stellar,

Ethereum Classic, Ox and the stablecoin USD Coin (USDC). The possibility of exchanging virtual currencies with fiat currencies should be noted.

Another important aspect to take into consideration when talking about Coinbase Pro is the ease of use of the platform, which is also valid for those who are new to cryptocurrency trading.

Kraken

Kraken was born in 2011, a year earlier than Coinbase. It owes its popularity to the rich fiat currency exchange section for Bitcoin (users can choose between euro, dollar, pound, yen, etc.).

The Kraken exchange currently supports 17 cryptocurrencies. These include Bitcoin, Bitcoin Cash, Bitcoin SV, Ethereum, Ethereum Classic, Ripple, Litecoin, Moreno, EOS, ZCash, DASH, Dogecoin and the stablecoin Tether.

Among the negative sides of Kraken we can mention the arbitrary closure of some accounts managed by normal users, as witnessed by some traders who spoke controversially about the platform founded by Jesse Powell almost ten years ago.

The availability of cryptocurrencies is greater than CoinbasePro, and the ability to exchange fiat currencies for virtual currencies is what makes it attractive for new crypto enthusiasts. However, the slower speed of operations compared to other equally famous exchanges and a question mark on security in light of the complaint relating to the arbitrary closure of some accounts does not give us the confidence to suggest it to those just starting out in crypto.

Bitstamp

Bitstamp was founded in the same year as Kraken (2011) by the very young Nejc Kodrič and Damijan Merlak. Born in 1989, Kodrič created Bitstamp at the age of 22. The exchange, whose base today is in Luxembourg, was created as a European alternative to Mt. Gox, the historic cryptocurrency exchange site that failed in 2014 (until a few months earlier it held 70% of Bitcoin transactions globally).

One of the main features of Bitstamp is the lower commission value compared to other competitors. For example, the commission on an international bank transfer is 0.05%, while for a withdrawal, 0.09% is the requested fee.

However, like CoinbasePro, Bitstamp does not allow traders to trade a large number of cryptocurrencies. At the moment, exchanges of Bitcoin, Bitcoin Cash, Litecoin, Ethereum and Ripple are allowed.

Bittrex

Bittrex is among the 5 best cryptocurrency exchanges along with the most well-known platforms mentioned so far. Its base is in Seattle, in the United States of America, and this makes Bittrex one of the safest exchanges for traders (in Washington State, security is a central theme in the debate related to the management of virtual currencies).

On Bittrex, only the exchange between cryptocurrencies is allowed, therefore it is not the ideal choice for those who instead aim to exchange between fiat and virtual currencies. The cost of commissions should also be emphasized, the percentage of which on average reaches 0.25%.

Based on its structure, Bittrex is also the platform where the largest number of cryptocurrencies are present. The list also includes Bitcoin, Ethereum, Ripple and Cardano.

Our insight into the best cryptocurrency exchange sites ends here. We remind you that new exchanges are born every day, but we advise you to just use the ones mentioned in this chapter. In fact, the cryptocurrency world is famous for the huge number of scams. Be cautious and everything will be fine.

Chapter 5 - Storing your Bitcoin

Now that you have learned where to buy your first bitcoin, it is time to store it properly. In fact, once the purchase is complete you do not want to leave your coins on an exchange. By now you should know that if you do not own the private key, you cannot say you actually own your bitcoins. Therefore, it is important to have a reliable place where you store and accumulate your coins for the future.

In this chapter we are going to take a look at some of the most entrusted cryptocurrency wallets. Let's start with the one we personally use to store our bitcoins: the Ledger Nano X

Ledger Nano X

In the next few pages we will consider all the important aspects to know, including the price of the Ledger Nano X. We will also see how to use it to keep your cryptocurrencies safe, keeping them offline in a device that completely protects them from any cyber attack. This system, we remind you, is the only one that is truly reliable: the online wallets of exchanges, even the most famous ones, are connected to the internet and are consequently exposed to cyber attacks.

Hardware wallets, on the other hand, only connect when you need to perform operations and remain completely inaccessible for the rest of the time. In addition to not being able to be attacked from the outside, hardware wallets also protect you against the possibility that you lose your device.

Thanks to a password system that identifies you in a unique way, in fact, if you lose your Ledger Nano X you just need to buy another one and recover all your virtual currency assets.

The device is even more compact and lighter than the previous ones, with its just 34 grams of weight that make it more pocketable than a normal USB stick. The package includes the following.

- The device;
- A USB cable for connecting it to a computer or smartphone
- The illustrated sheet with instructions for using the Ledger Nano X;
- A strap to hang the device and possibly carry it around the neck;
- Three sheets for recovering passwords, with space to mark them and instructions in case of loss.

As you may imagine, nothing is missing in this top tier product. Ledger puts us in a position to learn how to use the device directly thanks to the instructions in the package and moreover it gives us all the tools to connect it to our electronic devices.

The soul of Ledger Nano X is BOLOS, the operating system developed by Ledger. The code is not open source, which means it cannot be customized by developers but it is also not accessible to possible attackers looking for bugs.

The company jealously guards every string of the BOLOS code, and indeed this intuition has proved very useful over the years for the security of its devices. BOLOS is already installed in the Nano X microchip, so there is no need to do any external installation by downloading to the computer and passing the software via USB cable.

This step, foreseen by some competing products, on the one hand allows everyone to download the firmware versions they prefer; on the other hand, unnecessarily exposing the hardware wallet to an internet connection increases the risk of compromise.

Ledger Nano X is compatible with computers running Windows 8 or later, and Apple devices running Mac iOS 10.9 or later. It also connects to mobile devices. In particular, you need Android 7.0 and iOS 9 to establish a successful connection.
Wanting to draw a dividing line, we can say that it is compatible with all operating systems released or updated after 2017. In any case we recommend that you check the characteristics of the system installed on your device to make sure it is compatible with Ledger Nano X.

Ledger Nano X can connect to your devices in two ways. First of all, as every other hardware walled, it is able to do this via USB cable. The novelty of this year, however, is the possibility of connecting the Ledger to your devices via Bluetooth as well.

When the company announced this feature, disputes immediately flared up. Bluetooth connections, in fact, are much easier to attack than those via the internet. If the device is already designed to stay connected to the network for the shortest possible time, the possibility of leaving it connected to Bluetooth for hours does not seem very coherent with the philosophy of cryptocurrencies.

However, Ledger has confirmed that the data transmitted via Bluetooth are public ones. This means that, even if stolen by someone, it cannot be useful in any way; all private cryptographic keys are unique and jealously guarded within the wallet, and never leave the device. When connected via Bluetooth or USB cable to a device, the Ledger Nano X acts like a piggy bank that can be used to receive or send cryptocurrencies.

Obviously, each device must be configured using dedicated software and personal passwords, so that even in the event of theft, no one can connect it to their computer and use it at will. Even in this case, however, the connected device remains shielded thanks to the dedicated application that filters the passage of information.

Thanks to this intermediation, all critical data is never transmitted outside the Nano X.

The new Ledger is compatible with over 1,100 cryptocurrencies, and software updates gradually widen the range of options. Despite this, only 100 types of different cryptocurrencies can be stored for each Nano X. While it is rare to find someone who needs to store more than 100 different crypto, it is still a limitation for some people who like to diversify their portfolios and act as a venture capitalist for cryptocurrencies.

To add a cryptocurrency, simply open the Ledger Live software from any device. Once the program is open, you will be asked to authenticate using your credentials, thus accessing the main panel with all the available functions. At this point you will have to go to the catalog of available crypto, choosing the one you are interested in adding to our wallet.

Once the application has been selected, its download will begin. The code will be transferred to your Ledger Nano X which, from that moment on, will be ready to host wallets of the selected cryptocurrency. To add your portfolio you will have to open the application and complete the process. You will be asked for the access keys to your wallet, and once this is done we will have correctly configured the storage on our device.

What is important to understand is that, technically, cryptocurrencies are not "sent" to the Ledger, as they are not transferred from one wallet to another. The only thing that changes is the information on the blockchain that says where those funds are kept.

In any case, for simplicity, we will continue to use the term "send" to make the subject clearer. Once you open the application, suppose it is that of Bitcoin, at the top you will find two buttons: "Send" and "Receive".

By clicking on "Receive" you will display a unique code that can be used as a destination address for sending your Bitcoins directly to the Ledger Nano X. At this point it will be sufficient to use this key as the address for sending your cryptocurrencies.

The procedure for sending varies depending on where you previously stored your tokens; if you buy them for the first time from an exchange, you can have them sent directly to the address that appears on the Ledger Nano X.

The procedure for sending cryptocurrencies is almost similar to the previous one, with the only difference that you will have to click on the "Send" button instead of the "Receive" button. Your offline wallet will ask you for the recipient wallet. Once entered, just click on the "Send" button to complete the procedure.

Thanks to the cryptocurrency applications on Ledger Nano X you have the ability to check your balance and your incoming and outgoing transactions at any time. In this way you can always have an overview of your assets and keep cash flows under control.

There are various online stores that sell the Ledger, but it becomes extremely important to be able to trust the retailer. Someone, in fact, could sell compromised devices with the aim of stealing the coins contained inside. In fact, it is sufficient to update the operating system and install one with specially written code, to achieve this malicious effect.

If you don't want to take any chances, we recommend you to buy it directly on the Ledger website (https://www.ledger.com/).

Trezor

Trezor is a hardware wallet that connects to your computer via USB port. It can stock, send and receive cryptocurrencies of different types, among which we can mention Bitcoin, Ethereum, Ethereum Classic, Litecoin, Namecoin, Dogecoin, Dash, Bitcoin Testnet and even ZCash.

It includes important security features, such as a password manager and also a two-step authentication. It can also be integrated with other very popular wallets, such as MyEtherWallet and Copay, to securely manage even the virtual wallets that you may have opened on these specific platforms.

Trezor is a hardware wallet with an essential design, small in size, easy to connect to your PC and which also comes with a small band that allows you to connect it directly to your keychain, making it even more comfortable to be carried around.

At the time of writing it is available in two different colors: black and white. On the front of the device you will also find a low resolution white on black display and the two buttons that you will need to go on with the operations or to cancel them.

It is also possible to interact with all or almost all of the major exchanges on the internet thanks to the software that is delivered together with the hardware wallet and above all thanks to the Google Chrome extension that Trezor makes available.

Trezor offers certainly adequate security with respect to the management of wallets that contain important quantities of cryptocurrency within them. First of all, it allows you to have a backup of the wallet with a 24-word passphrase that is generated during the installation phase. After the first installation, a PIN code must also be entered: any mistake in entering the PIN exponentially increases the waiting time for the next try. It means that it would take about 17 years to make 30 attempts.

With the 24-word passphrase it is possible to recover the wallet at any time, even if the trezor we bought should be lost or destroyed. Equally important to take into account is the possibility of integrating the recovery methods even with virtual wallets such as Electrum. This is a feature the Ledger Nano X does not have.

Another important security feature concerning Trezor is the fact that to approve a transaction the keys on the hardware wallet must necessarily be pushed. This means that even in the very unlikely case that someone should enter your Trezor remotely, they will not be able to approve transactions without your consent.

The privacy profile for TREZOR is also interesting. In fact, we are faced with a device that has no serial code and therefore cannot be traced by anyone, much less by the manufacturer. This is a huge advantage in a world, that of cryptocurrencies, where user tracking is unfortunately a reality for almost every type of service that you can use.

Once you have purchased it, nobody will be able to associate your Trezor with your order. It is also worth mentioning that Trezor is also compatible with the large of the most popular software wallets in the world, among which we can mention Electrum, GreenAddress, Multibit, Mycelium and also with the software wallet offered by myTREZOR.com

It is also worth remembering what the technical specifications are as communicated by the manufacturer.

- Weight: 12 grams
- Size: 6 x 3 x 0.6 cm
- CPU: ARM Cortex M3 at 120 MHz
- Display: 128 × 64 pixel OLED Bright
- Connectivity: Micro USB
- Supported systems: Windows, Mac, Linux, Android

Furthermore, the Trezor source code is available on github, with the parent company inviting anyone with interest and ability to modify the code and to propose the aforementioned changes to the mother line of the firmware code as well.

This is a great opportunity for those who would like to know more about cryptocurrencies and programming even on an exquisitely more technical level. If for whatever reason you do not want to get a Ledger Nano X, then the Trezor is definitely the second best hardware wallet there is right now.

Chapter 6 - The Proof of Keys Day

As we have seen in the previous chapter, keeping your private keys safe is essential to ensure financial independence. Unfortunately, many cryptocurrency investors entrust their money exclusively to exchanges. This practice is far from safe, considering that exchanges have full control over cryptocurrency deposits.

Since the early days of Bitcoin, billions have been lost due to scams and cyberattacks against exchanges. The hack of the Mt.Gox exchange in 2014 is one of the most famous and controversial cases, and is still under investigation today.

The idea for the Proof of Keys was created by Trace Mayer, a podcaster and cryptocurrency investor. He created the concept as an annual celebration with the aim of encouraging investors to reclaim their monetary autonomy.
As discussed above, many people leave their cryptocurrencies on exchanges. This practice is inherently dangerous as these exchanges have full control over the private keys of the deposit addresses.

In this context, the Proof of Keys day aims to prevent investors from relying on exchanges for storing their cryptocurrencies. The concept is often presented with a short but effective motto: not your keys, not your Bitcoin.

The first Proof of Keys day took place on January 3rd, 2019 - the day of the 10th anniversary of the genesis block on the Bitcoin network.

In other words, Proof of Keys day celebrates financial sovereignty. Its goal is to encourage cryptocurrency investors to move their funds from exchanges to personal wallets. By taking full control over our private keys, we are assured that no one but us can access our funds.

Results of the Proof of Keys day

The philosophy behind the Proof of Keys day is perfectly in line with that of Bitcoin. By replacing third-party intermediaries with a trustless system for the transfer of value, individuals can confidently cooperate with each other - without giving up their monetary autonomy.

New investors learn how to move their coins

Cryptocurrency investors should be comfortable moving cryptocurrencies from place to place. While this may seem simple to some, beginners often find it difficult to understand the different types of wallets and how to use them.

For this, the Proof of Keys day encourages investors to learn more about the different types of crypto wallets and to practice their use. It is also a reminder of how value is transferred within decentralized blockchain networks.

Remind investors who really owns the private keys

As already mentioned, the central mission set by Trace Mayer at the origin of the Proof of Keys day was to encourage every cryptocurrency investor to own their own private keys. Leaving cryptocurrencies on an exchange means you have zero control over your own funds.

Even if it only happens once a year, Proof of Keys day is an opportunity for every investor to take control of their funds. While this day is a great warning about who owns what, it means very little if investors don't go all out in protecting their coins.

Unmasking shady or dishonest exchanges

Financial institutions are famous for the practice known as fractional reserve. In essence, it is a system that allows institutions to leverage existing deposits by lending more money than they actually own. Unfortunately, this is risky for the depositor, as a "bank run" could lead to bankruptcy.

In the context of the crypto sector, Proof of Keys day can encourage thousands of investors to withdraw their funds from exchanges. If a large percentage of investors decide to do this on the same day, they could eventually reveal exchanges that practice fractional reserve methods or are lying about their reserves.

Fortunately, the transparency of Bitcoin and other blockchain networks offers exchanges a very simple way to make their funds publicly verifiable.

Celebrating the genesis block of Bitcoin

Last but not least, Proof of Keys day is a way to celebrate the first block mined on the Bitcoin network. This block is known as the genesis block. The genesis block contains the first Bitcoin transaction made, in which Satoshi Nakamoto sent 50 BTC to Hal Finney.

Another memorable transaction took place on May 22nd, 2010, when two pizzas were bought for 10,000 bitcoins. The episode is now known as the Bitcoin Pizza day.

How to participate in the Proof of Keys movement

It doesn't matter if you are a newcomer or a veteran in the field of cryptocurrencies. Taking part in the Proof of Keys day is very simple. As we have already said, the idea is to declare financial autonomy by withdrawing all funds from exchanges (or other third party services).

First of all, you can take an inventory of all the funds you own on cryptocurrency exchanges. This will give you an idea of who really owns what when it comes to your bitcoins and altcoins.

Then, find a cryptocurrency wallet that you are comfortable with. In addition to ease of use, it is important to consider the security level of each type of wallet before making your choice. Finally, send your funds to your personal wallet to own and control your private keys.

Some people participate in the Proof of Keys movement once a year, moving funds off exchanges for one day on January 3rd to celebrate and affirm their financial sovereignty.

This practice is common among active traders, who must hold funds on exchanges in order to trade. Then, after the celebration, they move the funds back to exchanges. However, long-term investors who do not trade in the short or medium term should keep funds on a personal wallet until they decide to sell their coins.

Proof of Keys day is a simple but important event that reminds cryptocurrency investors who really owns their private keys. Millions of crypto enthusiasts join the celebration, moving funds off exchanges to their personal wallets.

As the blockchain industry grows, events like Proof of Keys day will not only help educate the community on the importance of private key ownership, but also on security principles in general.

Chapter 7 - Bitcoin Futures

In the previous chapters we always talked about buying "physical" bitcoins. However, the financial world is incredibly fascinating and has the ability to create financial instruments that are extremely complex and have no direct contact with "reality". Since this book is about Bitcoin, we feel it is extremely important to talk about the less known possibilities you have to interact with this asset. Therefore, in the next few pages we are going to cover everything you need to know about futures.

Many people are wondering how bitcoin futures work. From a strictly technical point of view, these are normal futures contracts, as they have been in the financial markets for a long time. Their peculiarity lies in the fact that they have BTC as an underlying asset.

In fact, futures contracts are precisely contracts between two parties for the purchase or sale of goods at a future date, or on expiration, and at a specific price agreed between the parties themselves. Upon expiry of the contract, the parties are in fact obliged to honor the agreements, buying and selling at the previously agreed price, regardless of whether the price of the underlying asset may have decreased or increased in the meantime.

They are used as a kind of insurance against the risks of price fluctuations. However, very often they are used to speculate as well. They are also exchangeable, i.e. once a futures contract has been issued it can be sold on the market by the parties who have signed it. When a futures contract is signed between two parties, one agrees to buy and the other agrees to sell. Those who decide to buy the underlying are said to open a long position, while those who decide to sell are said to open a short position.

Futures contracts were created specifically for the exchange of commodities, but in fact they can be used to trade any asset, including purely financial assets, such as bitcoin or other cryptocurrencies.

Bitcoin futures can be used to protect yourself from significant fluctuations in the value of BTC, but in reality very often they are used to speculate on the price of BTC without actually owning the coins.

Furthermore, many exchanges that allow BTC trading are not fully regulated, while those that allow BTC futures trading, such as ICE or CME, are fully regulated. Futures allow trading even for those who do not trust unregulated exchanges, or those institutional investors who simply cannot invest in markets that are not fully regulated.

Each single contract contains a certain volume of the underlying asset, and in the case of bitcoin futures this volume is usually 1 BTC. There are also futures contracts based on physical bitcoins, such as those of Bakkt, and others based on indexes that replicate the price, such as those of the CME.

Those not based on physical bitcoins are settled in cash, i.e. at maturity the exchange takes place in normal fiat currencies, and not in BTC. Since the first bitcoin futures contracts were placed on the market in December 2017, their success has gradually grown, so much so that the trading volumes in recent periods have begun to be significant.

Indeed, to tell the truth on those platforms where it is possible to exchange both physical bitcoins and bitcoin futures contracts, the trading volumes of the latter tend to significantly exceed those of real BTC exchanges, precisely because of the characteristics peculiar to futures, which allow very easy exchanges and within the reach of even the most demanding investors. This is a feature that is not only valid in the bitcoin market, but also in those of other commodities. However, remember that when you are trading futures, you never own the actual underlying asset.

What makes futures so speculative is the possibility to use leverage. Let's discover what it is and what it involves.

Leverage

Leverage is a tool that allows you to increase exposure on a financial market for a relatively modest capital investment. It is undoubtedly one of the most important features of trading with futures. When you invest in a leveraged product, the exchange will ask you to deposit only a small portion of the total position value. The remaining part of the capital will be made available by the exchange itself.

However, your profit or loss will be based on the entire exposure. So the amount you gain or lose may seem very high compared to the capital actually invested. It may even exceed your initial investment. This is the key concept of leverage and what attracts most cryptocurrency enthusiasts.

The initial outlay is called the margin or deposit requirement. Your provider will require it to cover, in whole or in part, any losses you could potentially incur. The margin is usually a small part of the entire exposure and its value depends on various factors. For instance, a more liquid and less volatile market requires a lower margin (eg 5%) than a volatile and less liquid market.

Some products require fixed margins per single contract, while in other cases the margin is calculated as a percentage of the position value.

How leverage works

Let's start with an example that clarifies doubts. If a particular market requires a margin of 10%, it means that by investing only 100 dollars you can get exposure on an investment of 1000 dollars. The leverage is therefore equal to 10 times the value you invested or, as they say in technical jargon, the leverage is 10:1.

Suppose you want to buy 1 bitcoin futures contract. If the current price is 60 euro, the transaction would cost you 60,000 dollars. If the price rises by 2000 dollars per contract, you can close your position at 62,000 dollars.

However, some exchanges offer you the opportunity to buy the shares of a bitcoin futures contract using leverage, simply by paying a margin (i.e. a percentage of the entire sum of 6000 dollars) in exchange for a total exposure.

Let's say the initial margin requirement is 10%. You will pay 10% x 60000 dollars x 1 contract = 6000 dollars. And if the share price were to rise from $60,000 to $62,000 you would make the same profit ($2000) as a non-leveraged transaction.

You made the same profit in both cases, but using leverage you only had to shell out a deposit of $6000 instead of the full $60,000. Your return was 100%, far greater than the 20% you would have achieved by buying the contract directly.

Although leverage is an excellent financial tool, it is still advisable to always remember that it amplifies not only the potential profits but also the losses, which can sometimes even exceed the initial deposit in the event that the market moves significantly against you.

Benefits of leverage

The main advantage of leverage is that it allows you to keep more liquidity in your portfolio, as you only have to tie up a small portion of the capital. You can also make the most of your capital and perhaps invest in a number of different assets rather than just one or two, diversifying your portfolio. However, it should be remembered that by operating with leverage you renounce all the advantages deriving from the actual ownership of bitcoin. It is also essential to remember that you may be required to pay additional margin to cover your losses should the market move in a direction that is unfavorable to you.

Who should use leverage

Investors and traders use leverage to amplify their exposure to various markets. This allows them to keep more liquidity in their portfolios to devote to other investments, diversifying their capital better than they could have done by physically purchasing the assets. You can use leverage on most cryptocurrencies on Binance.

Companies also use leverage to invest in assets from which to derive a relatively high return. A popular business strategy is to use debt to finance assets. This is because companies believe they can derive from these investments more than the cost of the interest they have to pay on their debt.

The effect of financial leverage

You must always bear in mind that leverage amplifies the scope of both gains and losses. While you have a good chance of making substantial profits, your potential losses are not limited to the initial deposit. The maximum loss, expressed as a percentage of the investment, is higher when you trade with leverage. However, it should be noted that the maximum risk, i.e. the highest amount you could lose, is the same whether you buy the assets for their full value or pay only a margin.

It is therefore important that you think in terms of the total position value and not just the margin you anticipated. You should therefore not make a leveraged investment without being prepared to fully cover any losses.

6 Advantages of Bitcoin futures

According to some experts, trading with Bitcoin futures could also be the best way to bet on the most widespread cryptocurrency in the world. Here are the six main reasons why some believe this to be the case.

1 Futures exchanges are managed by market experts

The creators of Bitcoin invented the blockchain, a cutting-edge technology that promises to revolutionize the world. However, they are not experts in creating markets. The CME and the CBOE both have a long experience in creating futures contracts for buying and selling. The launch of these trading venues will improve price management. This means that any new Bitcoin information will be quickly reflected on the contract price.

2 Large financial companies are familiar with futures

Wall Street firms are familiar with futures exchanges and how they work. Most of these carry out back-office operations that allow you to easily trade such instruments. This ease of use will attract more dollar volume on Bitcoin-related contracts. As a result, the Bitcoin futures market will become very liquid, perhaps more liquid than Bitcoin itself. For instance the SPDR S&P500 ETF is more traded than the underlying stocks in the index and a similar dynamic could also occur on Bitcoin futures.

3 The reference price

Contracts will be settled on each trading day using a transparent reference price. The reference price may not be perfect, but it will soon be written in contracts that provide for the payment or receipt of Bitcoin as is the case in other markets. For example, jewelry manufacturers and retailers often use gold reference prices in their contracts. In short, having a transparent settlement price will simplify the issue of using Bitcoin as a payment method.

4 Futures contracts are not lost

You can lose money on it, but you will never lose a futures contract. On cryptocurrency exchanges, however, it has already happened that Bitcoins were lost or stolen.

5 You can bet on the price drop

Going short on a futures contract is as simple as buying it. Those who believe that the Bitcoin price is in a speculative bubble can thus bet on a deflation of prices.

6 It is a regulated market

The Commodity Futures Trading Commission (CFTC) regulates futures trading. Those who love Bitcoin because it is not a government currency will not agree that regulation is an advantage. However, it's a significant plus for Bitcoin fans in general. The good news is that CFTC rules aren't as tough as those for stocks and bonds. What it does is introduce some rules that all market participants must adhere to and sets a level playing field for all speculators and investors who expose themselves to futures contracts. This feature will attract professional traders and thus increase the trading volume in the market. More trading volume will be beneficial for Bitcoin fans because it will make cryptocurrency futures a significant financial instrument, and consequently Bitcoin itself as well.

Chapter 8 - Bitcoin Options

Now that you understand the fundamentals of bitcoin futures, we can discuss an even more complex financial instrument. We are talking about options.

So mistreated by retail investors and yet so used by large investors on traditional markets, bitcoin options are a great tool to hedge spot positions.

In this chapter we will try to clarify what they are and we will try to demonstrate that the bad reputation they enjoy in the eyes of the general public is actually unfounded and that on the contrary, if used correctly and consciously, they possess characteristics that make them tools. very useful to enrich your arsenal of investment and trading strategies.

To do this, let's start by clarifying the basic concept, which however many manage to make complicated right from the start.

How do options on Bitcoin work?

The option can actually be considered as an insurance on the asset you hold, Bitcoin in your case, against a particular scenario that you think or fear may occur. To have this possibility, you pay an initial sum (exactly as you pay the insurance premium at the time of stipulation), high or low depending on the probability that the scenario has to come true. And exactly as in the case of an insurance, the option also has an expiry date, at the choice of the purchaser, beyond which it is no longer valid and can be exercised by the holder.

If your vision is a rise in the price of bitcoin, you will buy an upward option that "protects" you from a price increase beyond a certain value and will allow you to buy BTC in the future at a cheaper price (strike price). This type of option is called the CALL option.

If, on the other hand, your view is bearish, you will buy a bearish option that protects you from a decrease in the value of bitcoin below a value of your choice (always called the strike price). This option is called PUT.

And now the question that arises spontaneously: "but if my vision is bullish, why not buy Bitcoin right away before the price goes up? And if it is bearish, why not sell now?"

Well, the advantage of the option is precisely this. It gives you the opportunity to delay the decision to a future moment. If you were right, the insurance / option will make you collect the price difference between the value decided at the time of stipulation and the actual value on the day of sale (or expiry of the option). Otherwise, the option expires and you will have lost the premium paid initially. It should be emphasized that, as in the case of an insurance, the maximum loss is the sum paid on stipulation.

There is no liquidation risk, so much so that no maintenance margin is required for the purchase of options and there is no additional "hidden" outlay in addition to the initial one for the purchase.

Where to buy options

Certainly the first market to be mentioned in this sense is the CME, Chicago Mercantile Exchange, where futures and related options are listed on traditional financial markets. From 2020 the options on Bitcoin have also been added. The same goes for the BAKKT platform which is part of the ICE group. However, trading in these markets is only open to institutional and professional investors. A common investor looking to buy

Bitcoin options has to rely on other types of platforms. Almost all exchanges offer the possibility to buy futures, but not options on Bitcoin, whose trading is currently the prerogative of Binance, FTX, Deribit, Okex and LedgerX only.

While as far as futures are concerned, all exchanges provide similar, if not identical, services, for options the situation is different. In fact, Binance and FTX provide a service only on demand, i.e. there is no market with a book consisting of bids and offers such as we are used to seeing, but it is necessary to request a particular option with the desired characteristics and expect a quotation from the exchange itself or from another user of the platform willing to sell it to us.

This type of transaction can be defined as OTC, i.e. each option is tailored to the applicant and is only recommended for expert users who know what they are doing, as this type of market is less liquid and less transparent.

Instead, Deribit, Okex and LedgerX offer a type of negotiation similar to that of any crypto or crypto futures. Therefore, they are standardized, complete with a buy and sell book, and the same characteristics for each market participant. This feature makes buying, selling, and understanding what you are doing much easier.

If you are a beginner, we advise you to stick to the basic strategy of buying and selling spot bitcoins. In fact, futures and options are two extremely complicated financial instruments and should be used only by those that have some trading experience.

Chapter 9 - The Best Way to Accumulate Bitcoin

We have already written a book on Bitcoin and cryptocurrency trading, where we encourage readers to master the art of buying high and selling low. This time around, since we are talking to a lot of beginners, we would like to suggest a complementary approach to active trading.

In fact, active trading can be stressful, challenging and still yield poor results. However, there are other options available. Like many investors, you may be looking for a less demanding and time-consuming investment strategy. Or you prefer a more passive investment style. You have many options in the cryptocurrency ecosystem, including staking, lending your assets, participating in mining pools, and more.

But what if you want to invest in the markets but don't know where to start? More precisely, what would be the optimal way to develop a long-term position? In this chapter, we will discuss an investment strategy known as a DCA, or dollar cost averaging, which offers an easy way to mitigate some of the risks involved in opening a position.

What is DCA?

Dollar cost averaging is an investment strategy that aims to reduce the impact of volatility on the purchase of assets. It consists of buying equal amounts of the asset at regular intervals.

The premise is that by entering the market in this way the investment may be less affected by volatility than entering with a single big purchase. Why? Because buying at regular intervals can level out the average price. In the long run, such a strategy reduces the negative impact a bad income can have on your investment. Let's see how the dollar cost averaging strategy works and why you might want to consider using it.

The advantages of dollar cost averaging

The main benefit of dollar cost averaging is that it reduces the risk of placing a bet at the wrong time. Market timing is among the most difficult elements when it comes to trading or investing. Often, even if the direction of a trade is correct, the timing may be wrong - which makes the whole trade inaccurate. The capital accumulation plan helps mitigate this risk.

If you divide your investment into smaller portions, you are likely to get better results than investing the same amount of money in one block. Making a purchase with bad timing is surprisingly easy, and can lead to less than ideal results. Additionally, you can eliminate some of the preconceptions from your decision-making process. When you rely on dollar cost averaging, the strategy will make the decisions for you.

Dollar cost averaging, of course, does not completely mitigate the risk. The idea is just to make market entry smoother to minimize the risk of wrong timing. Capital accumulation plans are by no means a guarantee of a successful investment - other factors must also be taken into consideration, such as the duration of the investment and the asset you are investing in.

As we have already said, finding the right moment in the market is extremely difficult. Even the greatest veterans of trading sometimes struggle to read the market. Therefore, if you entered a position using the dollar cost averaging strategy, you may also need to consider your exit plan, a trading strategy for exiting the position.

Now, if you've determined a target price (or price range), this can be pretty straightforward. Again, you will need to divide your investment equally and start selling them once the market approaches your target. This way, you can mitigate the risk of not going out at the right time. However, this is entirely up to your individual investing system.

Someone adopts a "buy and hold" strategy, where essentially the goal is never to sell, as the value of the purchased assets is expected to continue to rise over time. Check out the Dow Jones Industrial Average's performance over the past century below.

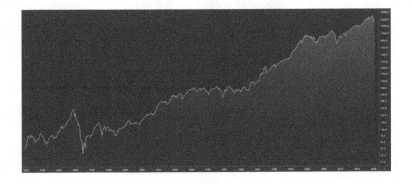

Despite the presence of short periods of recession, the Dow has been in a continuous uptrend. The purpose of a buy and hold strategy is to enter the market and stay in the position long enough to eliminate the importance of timing.

However, it is important to point out that this type of strategy is usually stock market oriented and may not be applicable to cryptocurrency markets. Remember that the Dow's performance correlates with a real-world economy. Other asset classes will perform very differently, especially if they are exclusively supported by speculation. We are not saying that this is the case for Bitcoin. On the contrary, in this case a dollar cost averaging strategy works very well.

Examples of dollar cost averaging strategies

Let's look at this strategy through an example. Let's assume you have a fixed amount of $10,000 dollars, and we think investing in Bitcoin is a reasonable bet. You also believe the price has a good chance of staying in the current zone, which is a good point to build up and develop a position using a dollar cost averaging strategy.

You could split the $10,000 into 100 $100 parts. Every day, you will buy $100 worth of Bitcoin no matter what the price is. In this way, you will distribute your income over a period of approximately three months.

Now, let's try to demonstrate the flexibility of dollar cost averaging with a different plan. Let's assume that Bitcoin has just entered a bear market, and that it will be at least two years before a sustained bull trend. However, you do expect a bull trend eventually, and you would like to prepare in advance.

Should you use the same strategy as before? Probably not. In fact, this investment portfolio has a much longer time horizon. Your $10,000 would remain allocated to this strategy for a few more years. So what's the plan?

You could split the investment back into 100 $100 parts. However, this time around, you will be buying $100 worth of Bitcoin every week. There are around 52 weeks in a year, so the whole strategy will run over a span of nearly two years. In this way, you will develop a long-term position as the downtrend takes its course. You will not lose the train when the uptrend begins, and you have also mitigated some of the risks associated with buying into a downtrend.

Keep in mind that this strategy can be risky when you are buying into a downtrend. For some investors, it would be best to wait for the end of the downtrend to be confirmed to start entering. If they wait, the average cost will likely be higher, but on the other hand many of the downside risks will be mitigated.

Dollar cost averaging calculator

You can find a great calculator for Bitcoin dollar cost averaging plans by visiting www.dcabtc.com. You can specify the amount, the time horizon, the intervals, and get an idea of the progress of various strategies over time. You will see that in the case of Bitcoin, which is in a sustained long-term uptrend, the strategy would have worked consistently.

Below you can see the performance of your investment if you had only bought $10 worth of Bitcoin every week for the past five years. $10 a week doesn't seem like much, does it? In April 2021, you would have invested a total of around $2600, and your bitcoin stack would be worth around $70,000.

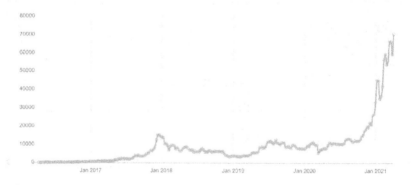

Chapter 10 - Bitcoin as a Store of Value

When we think of a safe asset, precious metals such as gold or silver probably come to mind. They are very popular investments as hedges against turbulence in traditional markets. The debate on Bitcoin's position in the footsteps of these assets is still on. In this chapter, we will look at some of the central arguments for and against Bitcoin as a store of value.

What is a store of value?

A store of value is an asset that can maintain its value over time. If you bought a good store of value today, you could be reasonably certain that its value will not decline over time. Going forward, you would expect the asset to have a similar (if not greater) value.

When you think of a "safe haven" asset of this type, you are likely to imagine gold or silver. There are a few reasons why these have traditionally held their value, which we will look at shortly.

The properties of a good store of value

To understand what the characteristics of a good store of value are, let's first explore those of a bad store of value. If we want to preserve something for long periods of time, it seems logical that it must be durable.

Let's consider food. Apples and bananas have some intrinsic value, as humans have to feed themselves to live. When food is scarce, these products will undoubtedly be very valuable, but that doesn't make them a good store of value. They will be of much less value if we keep them in a safe for several years, as they will obviously degrade.

Instead, let's consider something with an intrinsic value that is also durable, for example pasta. It is better in the long run, but there is still no guarantee that it will hold its value. Pasta is produced at low cost from readily available resources. Anyone can flood the market with new pasta, so pasta in circulation will see its value decrease as supply exceeds demand. Consequently, in order for something to hold value, it must also be scarce.

Some see fiat currencies (dollars, euros, yen) as a valid way to preserve wealth as they hold their long-term value. In reality, they are very bad stores of value because their purchasing power decreases significantly as new units are created (just like pasta). You can take your life savings and hide them under the mattress for twenty years, but they won't have the same purchasing power when you finally decide to spend them.

In the year 2000, with $100,000 you could have bought a lot more than you can today. This is mainly due to inflation, which refers to the increase in the prices of goods and services. In many cases, inflation is caused by an excessive supply of fiat currency resulting from the government's practice of printing new money.

To illustrate this phenomenon, suppose we own 25% of the total supply of $100 billion - hence, $25 billion. Time passes and the government decides to print, for example, another $800 billion to stimulate the economy. Our piece of the pie suddenly dropped to ~3%. There's a lot more money out there now, so it makes sense that our slice doesn't have the same purchasing power as before.

Like the pasta we mentioned earlier, dollars aren't expensive to make. What we have described above can take place within a few days. For a good store of value, it should be difficult to flood the market with new units. In other words, our slice of the pie should dilute very slowly, or not diminish at all. Taking gold as an example, we know that its supply is limited. We also know that it is very difficult to extract. So even if the demand for gold suddenly increases, turning on a printer isn't enough to create more. It must be extracted from the ground, as always. Even as demand grows, supply cannot be materially increased to satisfy it.

Bitcoin as a store of value

Since the early days of Bitcoin, its supporters have put forward the thesis that cryptocurrency is more like "digital gold" than a simple digital currency. In recent years, this narrative has been picked up by many Bitcoin enthusiasts.

The thesis of Bitcoin as a store of value states that this cryptocurrency is one of the most solid assets known to man. Proponents of the thesis believe that Bitcoin is the best way to preserve wealth over time by protecting it from devaluation.

Bitcoin is known for its incredible volatility. It might seem illogical how an asset that can lose 20% of its value in one day may be considered by many to be a store of value. However, even considering its numerous collapses, it remains to this day the best performing asset in history. So why is Bitcoin considered a store of value?

Bitcoin shortage

Perhaps one of the more compelling arguments for the store of value thesis is that Bitcoin has a limited supply. As you may recall from previous chapters, there will never be more than 21 million bitcoins. The protocol guarantees this property with a rule carved into the code.

The only way in which new coins can be created is in the mining process, in some ways analogous to gold mining. However, instead of drilling into the ground, Bitcoin miners must solve a cryptographic puzzle using computational power. By doing so they will earn new coins.

Over time, the reward decreases following events known as halving. As the name suggests, each halving halves the reward. In the early days of Bitcoin, the system distributed 50BTC to every miner that produced a valid block. During the first halving, this number was reduced to 25 BTC. The next halving halved it to 12.5 BTC, and the next one will cut the reward to 6.25 bitcoin per block. This process will continue for another 100+ years until the final fraction of the last coin is in circulation.

Let's create a model similar to the example we did earlier with our fiat currency. Suppose we bought 25% of the supply of Bitcoin (i.e., 5,250,000 coins) many years ago. When we acquired these coins, we knew our percentage would stay the same as there is no entity capable of adding more coins to the system. There is no government here - or rather, not in the traditional sense (more details soon). So, if we had bought 25% of the maximum supply in 2010, we would still have 25% today.

Decentralization

Maybe you are thinking, it is only open-source software. Everyone can copy the code and create their own version with 100 million more coins.

In fact, you could. Let's say you can clone the software, make the changes and run a node. Everything seems to work. There is only one problem, though: there are no other nodes to connect to. You see, as soon as you changed your software parameters, the members of the Bitcoin network started ignoring you. You have forked, and the program you are running is no longer what is globally accepted as Bitcoin.

What you just did is functionally the equivalent of taking a picture of the Mona Lisa and claiming that there are now two Mona Lisa. You can convince yourself that this is the case, but good luck convincing someone else.

We mentioned that there is some kind of government in Bitcoin. This government is made up of each user running the software.

The only way the protocol can be changed is with the majority accepting the changes.

Getting a majority to add coins would be no easy feat - after all, you're asking them to devalue their own funds. At present, even seemingly insignificant features take years to reach consensus across the network.

As it grows and gets bigger and bigger, promoting changes will get harder and harder. Therefore, holders can be reasonably sure that the supply will not be inflated. Even though the software is man-made, the decentralization of the network means that Bitcoin acts more as a natural resource than as code that can be arbitrarily modified.

The properties of good currencies

Proponents of the store-of-value thesis also point out characteristics of Bitcoin that make it a good currency. It is not only a limited digital resource, it also shares characteristics that have traditionally been adopted in the various currencies of history for centuries.

Gold has been used as a currency by several civilizations since their inception. There are several reasons behind this choice. We have already talked about durability and scarcity. These properties can create good assets, but not necessarily good forms of money. For this, fungibility, portability and divisibility are needed.

Fungibility

Fungibility means that the units are indistinguishable. With gold, you can take any two ounces, and they will have the same value. This also applies to things like stocks and cash. It doesn't matter which particular unit you own - it will have the same value as any other of the same type.

Bitcoin's fungibility is a thorny topic. It shouldn't matter which coin you own. In most cases, 1 BTC = 1 BTC. Things get complicated when we consider that each unit can be linked to previous transactions. There are cases where companies blacklist funds they believe have been involved in criminal activity, even if the holder received them later.

Should it matter? It is difficult to understand why. When you are paying for something with a banknote, neither you nor the merchant know what it was used for three transactions ago. There is no concept of a transaction history - new banknotes have no more value than used ones.

At worst, it is possible that older bitcoins (with a longer history) will sell for less than new bitcoins. Depending on who you ask, this hypothesis could be the biggest threat to Bitcoin or something you don't need to worry about. For now, however, Bitcoin is functionally fungible. There have only been a few isolated incidents involving frozen coins due to a historical suspicion.

Portability

Portability denotes the ease of transportation of an asset. $10,000 in $100 bills? Rather easy to move. $10,000 oil equivalent? A little less.

Sound money must have a small form factor. It must be easy to transport to allow individuals to pay each other for goods and services. Gold has traditionally been excellent in this area. At the time of writing, a standard gold coin holds a value of nearly $ 1,500. Many purchases worth a full ounce of gold are unlikely to be made, so smaller denominations take up even less space.

Bitcoin is indeed superior to precious metals when it comes to portability. It doesn't even have a physical footprint. You could keep trillions of dollars worth of assets on a piece of hardware that fits in the palm of your hand.

Moving gold worth one billion dollars (currently more than 20 tons) requires enormous effort and cost. Even with cash, you should be carrying several pallets full of $100 bills. With Bitcoin, you can send the same amount anywhere in the world for less than a dollar.

Divisibility

Another vital quality of money is its divisibility - that is, the ability to divide it into smaller units. With gold, you can take a one-ounce coin and cut it in half to make two half-ounce units. You may spoil the beautiful eagle or buffalo design on it, but the value of the gold remains the same. You can cut half-ounce units over and over to produce even smaller denominations.

Divisibility is another area where Bitcoin excels. There are only twenty-one million coins, but each is made up of one hundred million smaller units (satoshi). This gives users a high degree of control over their transactions, as they can send an amount by specifying up to eight decimal places. Additionally, Bitcoin's visibility makes it easier for small investors to buy fractions of BTC.

Reserve of value, medium of exchange and unit of account

The general opinion is divided on the current role of Bitcoin. Many believe that Bitcoin is simply a currency - a tool for moving funds from point A to point B. We will discuss this in the next section, but this perspective goes against what many proponents of the store of value thesis advocate.

Store of value proponents argue that Bitcoin has to go through various stages before becoming the definitive currency. It starts as a collector's item (probably the stage we are in now): it has proven functional and safe, but has only been adopted by a small niche. Its main audience consists of enthusiasts and speculators. Only with better education, infrastructure for institutions and greater confidence in its ability to retain value can it proceed to the next stage: the store of value. Some believe it has already reached this level, since institutions are investing in Bitcoin as well.

At this point, Bitcoin has not been widely spent due to Gresham's law, which states that bad money drives out good. This means that when presented with two types of coins, individuals will be prompted to spend the lower one and accumulate the higher one. Bitcoin users prefer to spend fiat currencies, as they have little confidence in their long-term survival. They prefer to keep their own bitcoins, as they believe they will hold their value.

If the Bitcoin network continues to grow, more and more users will adopt it, liquidity will increase, and the price will become more stable. Due to the increased stability, there will no longer be an incentive to keep it in the hope of big gains in the future. Hence, we can expect that it will be used a lot more in daily trading and payments, as a strong medium of exchange.

The increased use further stabilizes the price. In the final stage, Bitcoin would become a unit of account - it would be used to price other assets. Just as we could price a gallon of oil at $4, in a world where Bitcoin reigns as a currency we are going to measure this value in bitcoin.

If these three monetary milestones are met, proponents see a future where Bitcoin has become a new standard that replaces the currencies used today.

The case against Bitcoin as a store of value

The arguments presented in the previous pages may seem completely logical to some or completely absurd to others. There are some criticisms of the idea of Bitcoin as "digital gold" put forward by both Bitcoin enthusiasts and cryptocurrency skeptics.

Bitcoin as digital money

When disagreement arises on this issue, many are quick to point out the Bitcoin whitepaper. For them, it is clear that from the very beginning Satoshi designed Bitcoin to be spent. In fact, we find it in the same title of the document: "Bitcoin: A Peer-to-Peer Electronic Money System".

The argument suggests that Bitcoin can only be valid if users spend their coins. By accumulating them, you are not helping adoption - you are hindering it. While Bitcoin is not widely valued as digital money, its core proposition is driven not by utility but by speculation.

In 2017, these ideological differences led to a major fork. Bitcoiner's minority wanted a system with larger blocks, to offer lower transaction fees. Due to the growth in usage of the original network, the cost of a transaction can drastically increase, excluding lower value transactions for many users. If the average commission is $10, there is little point in spending coins on a $3 purchase.

The forked network is now known as Bitcoin Cash. The original network implemented an update around that time, known as SegWit. Segwit nominally increased the capacity of the blocks, but that was not his main goal. It also laid the foundation for the Lightning Network, which aims to facilitate low-cost transactions by moving them off-chain.

However, the Lightning Network is far from perfect. Regular Bitcoin transactions are much easier to understand, while managing Lightning Network capacity and channels has a steep learning curve. It remains to be seen whether it can be simplified, or whether the solution design is fundamentally too complex to rationalize.

Due to the growing demand for block space, on-chain transactions are no longer very cheap during busy times. For this, it could be argued that not increasing the block size damages Bitcoin's functionality as a currency.

No intrinsic value

For many, the comparison between gold and Bitcoin is absurd. The history of gold is, essentially, the history of civilization. Precious metal has been a staple of societies for thousands of years. Undoubtedly, it has lost some of its dominance since the elimination of the gold standard, but it remains the ultimate safe haven asset.

Indeed, the comparison between the network effects of the king of assets and a protocol that has been in existence for eleven years seems a bit too much. Gold has been revered for millennia as both a status symbol and an industrial metal.

Conversely, Bitcoin has no use outside its network. You can't use it as a conductor in electronics, nor can you work it to create a huge shiny chain when you decide to become a hip hop star. It might emulate gold (mining, limited supply, etc.), but that doesn't change the fact that it's a digital asset. In a sense, all currencies are a shared belief - the dollar only has value because the government says it and society accepts it. Gold is only valuable because everyone agrees it does. Bitcoin is no different at all, but those who value it are still a small group in the overall world of finance.

Volatility and correlation to other assets

Those who discovered Bitcoin in the early years have certainly seen their investment grow by huge orders of magnitude. For them, it has actually retained value - and more. However, those who first bought coins near the all-time high did not have this experience. Many have suffered large losses by selling at any later time.

Bitcoin is incredibly volatile, and its markets are unpredictable. Metals like gold and silver have insignificant fluctuations by comparison. You may argue that we are still in the early stages, and that the price will eventually stabilize. But this, in itself, would indicate that Bitcoin is not currently a store of value.

The relationship between Bitcoin and traditional markets must also be considered. Since the launch of Bitcoin, they have been in a constant uptrend. Cryptocurrency cannot truly be tested as a safe haven asset if all other asset classes are doing well as well. Bitcoin enthusiasts may refer to it as "unrelated" to other assets, but there is no way to know until other assets suffer while Bitcoin remains stable.

Tulipmania and Beanie Babies

It wouldn't be a real critique of Bitcoin's store-of-value properties if we didn't mention the comparisons to Tulipmania and the Beanie Babies. They are weak analogies at best, but they serve to illustrate the dangers of bubbles and their bursting.

In both episodes, investors flocked to buy items they thought were rare in hopes of reselling them for a profit. By themselves, the items weren't that valuable - they were relatively simple to produce. The bubble burst when investors realized they were massively overvaluing their investments, and as a result the tulip and beanie babies markets collapsed.

Again, these are weak analogies. Bitcoin's value comes from users' trust in it, but unlike tulips it cannot be grown to meet demand. That said, there is no guarantee that investors won't see Bitcoin as overvalued in the future, causing the bubble to burst.

Bitcoin certainly shares most of the characteristics of a store of value like gold. The number of units is limited, the network is decentralized enough to offer security to owners, and can be used to store and transfer value.

Ultimately, it has yet to prove itself as a safe haven - it is still too early to be certain. Things could go either way - the world could take refuge in Bitcoin in times of economic crisis, or it could continue to be used only by a minority group.

Only time will tell, but what we have seen since March 2020 is a progressive shift from bonds, gold and silver to Bitcoin and cryptocurrencies. We strongly believe Bitcoin is a store of value and we are dollar cost averaging into it on a weekly basis.

Conclusion

Congratulations on making it to the end of this book, we hope you found some useful insights to take your cryptocurrency trading skills to the next level. As you should know by now, the world of Bitcoin is extremely complicated and there is a new "opportunity" every way you look. However, our experience tells us that only by taking things seriously and having a proper plan you can develop your investing skills to the point that you can actually accumulate wealth.

Our final advice is to stay away from the shining objects that the world of cryptocurrencies offers you every day. Simply dollar cost average into Bitcoin and study the world of cryptocurrencies in depth. After you have sufficient knowledge on what you are talking about, you can go ahead and invest into other cryptocurrencies. Analyze your results, improve your money management skills and become the master of your emotions.

As you can see, there are no shortcuts you can take. Easy money does not exist. What exists is the possibility to start from zero and work your way up to become a professional Bitcoin investor. The journey might be difficult, but it is certainly worth it.

CPSIA information can be obtained
at www.ICGtesting.com
Printed in the USA
LVHW011942280421
685871LV00006B/114